ConcealHer No More

D'Author Nicole

Printed in the United States of America

First Printing, 2020

ISBN 978-1-7357976-0-1

The Author

D'Author Nicole, also known as Denise Nicole Backus, has endured emotional and physical scars for nearly fifty years. Ready to shed the scars that have mismanaged her well-being, the way she views herself and those around her, the pages of this memoir are a balm for Denise to break free from bondage and heal from past hurts and lingering pain. After several failed friendships and romantic relationships, D'Author Nicole embraces who she is, grateful for her husband and two sons who have supported her on this journey. No longer walking in shame and self-doubt, D'Author Nicole has worked to forgive herself for not being appreciative of the life she was blessed with. Now, she focuses on her blessings, without dwelling on her brokenness. This project is a labor of love for D'Author Nicole's healing, as well as assisting in the healing of others who may be suffering from the same adversities she faced in her past. Denise is working to rebuild trust in herself in order to continue to live a more harmonious life.

Acknowledgements

To God be the glory for the things He has done!

Thank you to my loving husband, Jimmie Backus Jr., and my sons, Bryson Connor Backus and Donovan Nigel Backus for not hesitating to hear my heart and most importantly, standing in agreement as I documented my story. I love you guys, and I am so blessed to unequivocally know that you love me back.

I'm grateful to my parents, who experienced my trauma before I truly knew it existed. I realize that raising me during and after the accident was tough, especially witnessing outsiders making a spectacle of your child while questioning some of the decisions you made. Nevertheless, you did the best you could, raising a child with a disfiguring facial scar. Dealing with your own emotions, you loved me through it all. I want you to know that I appreciate all the ways you made sure I experienced "normal" activities and opportunities, just as children without the scars I had.

To the women who helped manifest my "2020 vision" of connecting with other women, thank you. This connection - as you will read later in this book, became a huge part of my healing process. It was not my plan to be so transparent, at least not as early as it occurred, but being obedient and listening to God's plan gave me the strength to share sooner than I expected.

To the bold women who willingly volunteered to be a part of my project and reveal their scars, thank you. To my partners behind the scenes who helped me along the way with this book, from my writing coach, Lorna Lewis and her team, to the great graphics, marketing and photography women in the District of Columbia, Maryland, and Virginia (DMV) area, I thank each of you for believing in me and the power of my words. To my family, friends, and readers who encourage and support me, thank you. You are appreciated.

In memory of my loved ones who I know are proud of me even though they are not here on earth: - my grandparents Willie Seward and Sindia Louise Seward, my paternal grandparents, Jerry Walker and Mary Shadd Walker, and other family members, I miss you all and truly wish you could be here to celebrate my accomplishment. I am no longer concealing myself but instead, running towards the path of really being me.

Finally, I modestly thank myself for being brave enough to share the power of my scars, and the strength in words. Regardless of age, scars can control our lives if we allow them to. Scars are memorable, but they do not have to hold us in bondage. I encourage everyone reading this book to look beyond your scars with courage and heal.

Preface

Our experiences impact us more than we realize. Some say peace comes from acknowledging our experiences and the circumstances surrounding them. Finding peace means recognizing there are some things we will never understand or be able to explain, no matter how long we live. There are things in life we cannot control because they are a part of God's plan for our lives. Whether we're happy with His plan or not, we must learn to accept ourselves for who He has created us to be and receive the challenges He's prepared to help us overcome.

One Sunday, my pastor told our congregation, "God will create a crisis to develop your character because He is taking you somewhere." God is using my experiences to make me a better person. Though I am accustomed to helping and putting others first, I trust that I will be in a healthier position to aid others once I have broken free from my inadequacies.

Our unique qualities make us who we are. Each of our characteristics gives us purpose. It may take time to figure out what that purpose is, but moving forward takes courage. In order to advance, we must trust God and ourselves. Often, loving ourselves is a tough feat but it can be done. To do this, we must be willing to withstand the discomfort of digging deep and reliving past experiences. Though it's painful in the beginning, it makes us stronger in the end.

Each of us is responsible for our own happiness. Happiness is out there waiting for us to claim. When we begin taking steps towards freedom, we start living different lives, with distinct understanding and appreciation for our existence. Don't waste time on foolish thinking; believe God knew what He was doing when He created us, and when He allowed adversity in our path.

Don't compare yourself or your circumstances to others; we are all different and deserve to get the best results out of this thing called life. I never thought I would be sharing my personal experiences in a book made available for anyone to pick up and read. When I decided I was ready to share the intimate details which helped me deal with my insecurities, I realized I needed to be transparent to empower others like me. This book isn't simply about me – it's about my struggles as well as trials of others. It is a great reminder that we are never alone, because we all have adversities to work through.

Getting Started

First, let's embark upon this journey by accepting our scars. I have confidence in the influence of putting pen to paper. Writing gives clarity, and helps provide understanding about one's self and situations that occur in our lives. Additionally, writing relaxes your mind and allows your thoughts to flow freely to convey in a clear manner. As we start on the path to healing, ask yourself these simple, yet potentially complex questions:

1. What emotional scar(s) do you need or want to deal with? How have they affected your life?

[Handwritten response:] Really these days unkplace there, really present this.
— Warrior mode, define mode
— But up syther — age 22 can broke law

2. What physical scar(s) do you need or want to deal with? How were they caused? How have they affected your life?

[Handwritten response:] Physical scar is related to empowerment - transplant adjment

"IT" Controls Me

The morning started like any other, but that particular morning I was preparing to leave my family for a short while on a business trip. My Uber arrived 15 minutes later than scheduled to take me to the airport, and I panicked. Not only because I was already rushing to get to the airport on time, but because I couldn't remember if I packed "it." My heart began racing; pain surged through my stomach. I just knew I was going to vomit, because I was convinced I left "it" behind. Crippling scenarios raced through my mind; what would happen if I didn't have "it?"

I wanted to fall out and cry like a baby. That's how serious the situation was to me. There was no choice - I had to turn around. I couldn't risk getting on the plane without the one thing that could change my entire trip.

"Excuse me," I said to the driver.

"Yes, Ma'am?" he said, peering at me through the rearview mirror.

As soon as our eyes met, I knew I couldn't do it.

"Never mind." I said, tapping my fingers on my thigh.

I couldn't ask the driver to turn around and take me back home, like I wanted. We were already late and I couldn't miss my flight. Besides, the heavy Washington, D.C. metropolitan area traffic was too tight for me to go back. Living in the DMV meant leaving early to get anywhere on time; that's why I scheduled the Uber to arrive so early. I couldn't change traffic, nor could I change the fact that I still didn't know if I packed "it" or not. I took some deep breaths, willing myself to calm down. *There's nothing you can do about it now,* I repeated continuously in my head, trying to make myself be okay.

But I wasn't okay. Not at all.

The more I tried to take my mind off things, the worse I felt. Nothing was working - the deep breathing, meditating…nothing. At that point I did the only thing I knew to do next. What I should've done in the beginning. I whispered a prayer, trusting that the Lord wouldn't have allowed me to leave "it." Not only did I need to trust Him, but I needed to trust myself. Surely, I wouldn't have made a mistake like that. The more I prayed, the better I felt. The weight was lifted, but the heaviness remained. My flesh wouldn't stop wondering, "What if I did? What would I do?"

Maybe I'd run out and buy an emergency replacement once I arrived at my destination. I reassured myself once again, that everything would work in my favor. If I didn't have "it," there was time to buy more. I had the remainder of the day to take care of this situation, since my meeting wasn't scheduled until the next day.

That problem was solved, but then another issue popped in my head. I was going to be in a whole new state. What if those stores didn't carry the same products as my store back home? What if I couldn't purchase the exact item? What if I bought something similar and it didn't work? Everyone would know that something was wrong as soon as they laid eyes on me. They probably wouldn't say anything to my face, but there would be plenty of conversations behind my back. That's when the panic set in once again. I didn't know if I could do it. I wasn't ready to be exposed in that way. The bottom line was, I had to have "it." My anxiety was at an all-time high. It was bad enough to be stressed being away from home; I didn't need to pile this on my list of grievances.

Traveling for work was one of my least favorite things to do, especially during the fall, winter, and spring months. As a mother of two boys - my "sonshines" who mean the world to me, traveling was difficult when school was in session. Like most mothers I know, I'm the parent who handles most of the day-to-day activities with the boys, specifically schoolwork. Of course my husband was there to assist, but he didn't fully comprehend how to help, so I couldn't turn him loose with schoolwork or projects without thoroughly explaining what was expected first. Teaching him to help the boys was so taxing, I found it easier to handle their education myself, which worked out fine...until I had to leave town. Being away wasn't the problem - the heavy preparation to make it happen smoothly was.

With limited time being a major factor in my life, I usually began packing the night before I was scheduled to leave. Traveling didn't stop mom duties, so I learned to manage my schedule accordingly, juggling my sons' hectic schedules with mine. They attended different schools, so coordinating my boys' transportation to and from school was a major concern. Lunch schedules, projects, homework, quizzes, tests, and of course after-school sports and activities all had to be arranged before I hopped on the plane. Oh, and let's not forget I had to shop for groceries and fill the refrigerator for the week. I meal prepped so my husband and boys would have plenty to select from for dinner, cleaned the house and made it comfortable for my husband's benefit as well as my children.

Being a working mom, especially one who travels, means trying hard to make sure your home runs smoothly in your absence. Traveling is way more work than staying, but it comes with my duties. Believe me - I'm not complaining, I'm simply showing how I could've gotten so wrapped up in making sure everyone else was taken care of, that I overlooked the one thing that would take care of me. That thing which would make me feel comfortable and secure.

Normally when I pack, there are a few items I intentionally leave out to toss in my luggage in the morning right before I leave. Mostly toiletries, but one of those items is a must – it's very important to me. I may have forgotten things in the past, but this was one thing I never forgot.

6

Once we arrived at the airport, I almost didn't let the car come to a complete stop before jumping out because time wasn't on my side; there was a good chance I was going to miss my flight. I grabbed my luggage and raced to the terminal, trying not to fall with my rolling bag trailing behind me.

I got checked in and found a quiet spot to rummage through my bags, praying to find what I needed inside. I didn't really want to check, because I wasn't ready to find "it" missing, but checking my watch, I realized if I wanted to know, I had to look now. If I was going to have a breakdown, I'd rather it be while I was sitting alone than waiting until I was on a crowded plane.

I whispered another prayer, asking the Lord to please let "it" be there. That I would unzip the pocket that I kept "it" in and find "it" in its proper place. Staring ahead, I nervously opened my bag. I slid my hand inside, unzipped the side pocket, reached in, and there "it" was, right where I placed it…my concealer. Praise the Lord! Now, before you judge or confuse my concern with vanity, I assure you that it's a real issue for me. I would love to say I pack my concealer to hide a few blemishes here and there, but what I was hiding was something that had controlled my life for more years than I care to mention.

Time to Change the Game

I boarded my flight, filled with a new attitude and joy I hadn't felt since leaving home. I zipped my bag and sashayed to the plane, everything better. I settled into my seat and spent the entire flight reflecting on my near break-down. I realized that I had to make a change and get over my issue. I couldn't continue torturing myself.

I wish I could say this was the first time I freaked out about my concealer, but it wasn't. I panicked over it even when I wasn't traveling. I could be at home or running a quick errand, and if I wasn't wearing concealer, it felt like the secret I hid most of my life was exposed. I was completely naked without my concealer and that was a feeling I did not like experiencing. Trust me; I wish my life wasn't like that. I just wanted to be plain ole me. I despised allowing something so far out of my control to cause me to lose sight of who I am.

I have finally reached a point where I'm ready to reveal the real me. I'm ready to openly share my story with the masses because I believe there are many others who can relate. Most importantly I'm ready to release the bondage this thing has had over me.

For the first time, I'm truly ready to break free.

Writing this book wasn't exactly what I had in mind when I thought about sharing my story. Although I always wanted to write a book, I didn't know exactly what I would write about. In my mind, I imagined writing some twisted love story or a thriller filled with crime and mystery - things I enjoyed reading. Who knows, that may still happen somewhere down the road. I've always enjoyed writing, so the idea of writing a book wasn't far-fetched.

I did play around with the idea of writing a children's book. The main character would be a victim of bullying and I would share steps to overcome cruelty and insecurities at a young age. As I thought about the storyline, I realized that the child I wanted to write about was me. These were the steps I wish I had taken when I was bullied growing up. Working on that story dredged up pain I thought I'd dealt with, but it was clear I hadn't. It dawned on me that before I write a children's story to help others, I needed deliverance myself. I had to address my unresolved issues before unintentionally projecting them onto young readers.

It's my desire to be a stronger voice for readers by unveiling my true self. Being courageous on purpose. I will do a better job of embracing myself and empowering others with similar concerns to know they are enough. As it says in the book of Psalms, "I am fearfully and wonderfully made." Many of us have heard this scripture throughout the years, yet it amazes me how few of us believe it or even live it.

I'm one of those few.

Fearfully and wonderfully made. We recite this verse and teach it to others, but few of us who look at ourselves in the mirror and make the declaration truly accept it as truth. Most of us have something about ourselves we wish could change or improve. Unfortunately, I've allowed my imperfections to rule my life. Being fearfully and wonderfully made means accepting me for who I am. Loving me for who I am. It means not just reading the words, but believing and making them my reality. I know I'm not alone; many of you desire to do the same.

One of my favorite prayers is the Serenity Prayer:

God grant me the serenity to accept the things I cannot change, courage to change the things I can, and the wisdom to know the difference. Living one day at a time; enjoying one moment at a time; accepting hardships as the pathway to peace; taking, as he did, this sinful world as it is, not as I would have it; trusting that he will make all things right if I surrender to his will; that I may be reasonably happy in this life and supremely happy with Him forever in the next. Amen.

When I first heard this prayer years ago, it became my mantra. I'd recite it all the way up to *"wisdom to know the difference."* I read and focused on the entire prayer, repeating it over and over, trying hard to make it my personal affirmation.

…I failed day after day.

Accepting things for what they are can be so difficult. Realizing there are things I cannot control or change was disheartening. It took time to mature into these words. It wasn't an overnight process, nor did I expect it to be. I found my maturity when I took the step to no longer be held in captivity by the things I can't change.

Accident with Lasting Memories

Fifty-one years ago, there was a young married couple who made their home in New York. The woman was born and raised in Lawrenceville, Virginia; the man born and raised in Wedgefield, South Carolina. When the two married, she was in her early-twenties, and he was in his late-twenties.

On August 14, 1972, the young couple welcomed their daughter into the world. Many family and friends came to visit the little girl at the United Hospital in Port Chester, New York. After a few months passed, the mother and father had to face reality, as many new parents do. They had to return to work and make a living for their household. There was no way they could stay home and take care of their child all day – even if that's what they wanted so badly.

Someone had to care for their child while they were away.

One of their friends suggested a babysitter and the couple agreed, confident in their decision to hire the stranger to care for their child. After all, the woman was an experienced mother herself who looked after the children of others. Surely, she would care for

11

their child in the same manner or better than she cared for her own... or so they hoped. They had no way of predicting how their life and the life of their child was about to change in an instant.

The couple I'm referring to are my parents; the young child is me. Of course, I was too young to remember the details, so I'm documenting what was told to me once I was old enough to understand.

I don't know the exact date, but in February 1973, when I was six-months old, my parents received the phone call no parent ever want to receive. There was an accident; they needed to rush home. In a matter of hours, my parents' normal day ended in the emergency room, praying for my survival.

I'd suffered third degree burns.

According to the babysitter, I was asleep on the bed, which was beside a radiator. It was the middle of a bitterly cold New York winter; the radiator was lit and doing its job to heat the house. The sitter said since I was asleep, she felt confident that she could run to the bathroom and be back before anything could happen. Her assumption was wrong. She was gone a few minutes before hearing what she described as an excruciating scream, far from an infant's normal cry.

Somehow, I rolled off the bed and landed on the radiator. You wouldn't have to experience it to imagine how painful that must've felt. The accident left a scar on my face and wrist. My parents and everyone were so thankful that the scars were my only injuries. As a parent myself, I cringe thinking what must have gone through my parents' minds seeing me injured so badly. Imagining how it could've been worse; wishing they could take the pain from me.

I believe my parents felt assured that the scars I suffered would eventually fade and I'd go on to live the peaceful life they prayed I'd have one day. Everyone - my parents included, was concerned about my external scars, but it was the hidden ones which eventually caused my greatest pain.

Even though I'm no longer that baby girl, I still carry her scars.

Over the years, I felt like I was the only person who suffered the consequences from that accident. It seemed like everyone else was living a normal life, while I spent my time trying to conceal my shame. Time proved that I wasn't suffering alone. The accident left a huge impact on my parents as well. Though I'd attempted several times to talk with them about it, they were never truly ready. Instead of transparency, I was given the abridged version of what occurred.

My parents' way of dealing with my curiosity was by not giving attention to it at all. My one wish is that one day my parents will feel free enough to talk about the incident. Their silence caused me to internalize my thoughts and feelings. They don't know the pain and long suffering I've endured, and the energy I put into avoiding this topic with others because of their silence.

I tried to talk to my mother about it approximately 10 years ago.

"Mom, can we talk about the accident?" I asked.

She shook her head, catching me off guard. "I can't. I don't want to talk about it," she said dismissively

I expected to be disappointed, but the shame I felt when my mother denied me caught me by surprise. It seemed my scar was my family's dirty little secret, never to be mentioned. Mom's reaction caused me to shut down. If she reacted this strongly, I didn't even want to imagine how strangers would respond. All I focused on was the scar, without considering my parents' possible guilt and how discussing it caused them to relive one of the worst days of their lives.

They remembered what I couldn't.

It was unfair to all of us.

I never told my mother I dealt with hurt or shame all of these years…but having the strength to use the power of my voice and write this book, allowed me to open up to her. As a parent, now I understand how difficult it was to deal with the trauma that occurred. Times were different back in the 70's, where in many families - especially African American ones, things weren't talked out. There was a silent rule that situations were shoved under the rug like they never happened.

Not once did I ever doubt how much my parents loved me, or love me till this day. I don't blame them for leaving me with a sitter. I also don't blame them for their lack of communication about the accident. I believe my parents simply didn't know how to handle what happened to me and haven't been able to adequately explain to me how to handle the negativity attached to it.

In addition to protecting myself from the outside world, I also tried to protect my parents as well. There was no way to share my story without mentioning them. Not only was I protecting them from outsiders' backlash, I was shielding my parents from my negative emotions. I internalized thoughts and feelings I thought would be harmful to them rather than openly communicating.

My parents didn't deserve any more pain than they already felt.

Unlike my mother, until recently I hadn't attempted to speak with my dad about the incident. Even left unspoken, I was certain Dad hadn't released his pain, either. I realized I was right when I decided it was time to have the conversation my parents and I avoided all those years. They shared things with me they'd never shared before, and I was grateful for their transparency and memories.

A day before my 48th birthday and two days before making a public announcement about this memoir, I made the calls to my parents. I called them separately because I wanted to give them each an opportunity to express themselves without the other being present.

Mom was my first call.

"Hello," she answered in her usual cheery voice.

"Heeeeey," I responded with the nervousness of a five-year-old child. I mustered up the courage to continue. "You have a moment to chat?" I asked, unsure I truly wanted Mom's answer to be yes. I had to get it over with, but I was afraid that she still wasn't ready to discuss the accident.

"Yes, I am just running a few errands, what's up?" My mom's tone was so chipper, it made me feel bad because the talk we were about to have was going to bring her down.

"Well, I want to share something with you, and I've been having anxiety about it because I wasn't sure how you'd react. You may not know this, but I'm extremely self-conscious about my face," my voice cracked.

"I didn't know that it bothered you," Mom said. "Are you thinking about having surgery?"

"No, I'm not going to have surgery, but I am writing a book," I proudly announced. "There are so many people who don't know about my scar and I'm tired of hiding it and worrying about what they'd think. I'm writing a book about the accident and what I've been through as a result of it."

"A book? So, this is your ministry? Praise God, that's wonderful." Mom sounded excited.

"Well, I guess I could look at the book as a ministry because not only am I sharing about myself, but I've been reaching out to others with similar circumstances. It's past time for me to get over being uncomfortable. There are people here who've never seen me without my concealer."

"What?" Mom's voice went from excitement to shock. "You mean no one in Maryland has seen your face without makeup?"

"Other than those who knew me when I first moved here and a few others I've shared my story with, no." I answered matter-of-factly.

"I'm sure some of them have seen it because it doesn't totally vanish beneath the concealer," she pointed out.

"I know. A few people said they could tell something was there and others said they never noticed it."

"This is your ministry. We all have a ministry," Mom - who is a pastor, reiterated. "I didn't know this bothered you, I just wished it never happened."

Now that I told her about the book, it was time to dig a little deeper. "Can you tell me more about what happened that day? I don't remember you or daddy telling me about it directly. I just remember hearing you all answering questions when people asked what happened. I never told you about all the names kids called me. I guess in my own way, I believed I was protecting you from knowing I was being picked on. I figured you felt bad enough that it happened." My nerves calmed down after sharing so much of my heart.

"We never felt guilty, but definitely sorry it happened." Mom was quiet for a moment, as if remembering that day.

"Can you tell me where you were when everything happened?" I needed to be sure my recollection was accurate.

"I dropped you off that morning and went to work, and wasn't there long before I got the call. I only know what the sitter told us, which was that you rolled off the bed and fell on the radiator. It wasn't until I arrived to pick you up from her home that I found out it was your face that was affected. Just to see the raw skin, hurt so badly. We tried everything to make it better, to make it go away. The doctors said surgery wouldn't work at the time because there wasn't enough extra skin to use. I just wish it never happened. People always remarked how beautiful you were."

"I went to see a surgeon years ago and he said the same thing. I still didn't have enough skin to have cosmetic surgery," I shared, confirming what the doctor told her back in the day. "I knew I'd either have to find another way or learn to live with it. That's when I started wearing concealer."

We spoke a bit longer, and the conversation eventually led to a dream I had about my uncle, who's been deceased for years.

"I had a dream that I was back home in South Carolina preparing for a photoshoot for my book," I told Mom. "In the dream, I was telling you all about the book and stressed that I didn't want you all to tell anyone. Well, we arrived at the photoshoot, and I was upset that my secret got out. Then people said Daddy told them because he was so proud. I looked out amongst the crowd of people and there was Uncle Will and Junior (his son, my deceased cousin) smiling at me. It was really weird, but the only thing I could think of was how Uncle Will was always there. That dream caused me to think about the time I was young in the hospital. I had a wrapping around my head and face from surgery, and Uncle Will asked me if I wanted some ice cream or a milk shake."

"Oh yes, Will took it pretty hard," Mom said. He kept saying, "Her face, her face! Such a pretty girl and they messed up her face." Mom shared this fond memory of my dad's brother. "I think the dream is Will's way of confirming that it's time to let go of these feelings and do something about it."

After Mom and I chatted a while longer, we finally hung up, and I took a few minutes to digest our conversation.

Then I called Dad.

"Hello, how are you?" I asked when he answered the phone.

"I'm doing fine, on my way home from work." At the age of 79, he was still doing what he loved, farming.

"I called to tell you I'm writing a book and my focus is about the burn on my face. Can you tell me what you remember about that day?" I spewed the question because I knew Dad wouldn't allow this call to linger too long.

Dad was quiet for a moment before answering. "That morning, you were so frisky, you almost jumped out of the bed before we left home. Your mother called me at work, hysterical, telling me that you fell on the radiator at the babysitter's house."

Dad spent the next few minutes describing what a radiator was. I didn't bother telling him I knew all about radiators. It was then my father reminded me that I endured three surgeries following the accident. That was the memory I had of my face being wrapped and Uncle Will asking if I wanted some ice cream or a milkshake.

After a brief moment of silence, my dad continued, "The doctors removed the skin from your face because it was dead. He told us they could potentially perform one more surgery that would possibly leave one line on your face; however, they recommended that we wait until you were older to look into a skin grafting procedure. You didn't have enough skin to ensure a fourth surgery would be totally successful. Plus, by that time, we moved to South Carolina and your mom and I decided that we'd done the best we could do and it was best to leave your face alone without putting you through another surgery."

I found it interesting that their stories not only provided me with more clarity, but matched the information I received from the cosmetic surgeon I visited on my own years ago. It seemed that the answer we all received was to leave my beauty mark - my facial blessing, alone and handle it with style and grace.

My Young Life

When I was five years old, my family moved from New York to Sumter, South Carolina. Dad's love of farming wouldn't let him stay away any longer. He had land where he wanted to build a house, and was prepped for life as a full-time farmer. Ready to escape the hustle and bustle of the city, my mother - a country girl herself, was fine with the move.

I on the other hand, was not.

It was 1977, and we moved just in time for kindergarten. I was totally against relocating, determined to stay in Mamaroneck, New York in our two-bedroom apartment. What child wanted to move so far away from all the friends they'd ever known? My parents tried their best to appease me by saying, "You're going to love it in South Carolina," and "we'll have a new house, and there will be plenty of land to run and play." They even tried to convince me that I would make new friends and could come back and visit my old friends when possible.

When summer arrived, we hit the road with a trailer loaded with our belongings. We drove to South Carolina and stayed with my paternal grandparents while our four-bedroom ranch style home was being constructed. As promised, there was definitely plenty of yard space at our soon to be new home…but since I wasn't an outdoors kind of girl, the extra space meant nothing to me.

My parents enrolled me in a local elementary school, and we got acquainted with our new normal. Being the new girl and not knowing anyone made me shy and nervous. I wasn't prepared for the barrage of questions coming my way. The kids didn't ask what my favorite game was, if I had a favorite toy, or television show. There was a single interest that drew the children's curiosity about me:

How did I get this scar?

"What happened to your face?" some asked.

"What's that on your face," others chimed in.

These questions followed me throughout childhood, right into college. No matter how many times I was asked, I never learned how to properly respond to them. Had someone explained that people were asking because they were curious and not trying to hurt my feelings, I may have been more receptive. Even though the constant interrogations were aggravating, they were a lot better than the name calling I endured. Those were hurtful and unoriginal. Names such as "burn up face" and "Scarface" sent me to bed in tears at night.

I never told my parents how I was being treated. Maybe I intended to protect them; maybe I was too embarrassed to repeat the horrible names. I tried to suck it up and move on. Told myself that what the kids said was true. I did have a scar on my face and although my entire face wasn't burned, maybe "burn up face" fit who they saw.

Growing up as a farmer's daughter meant spending summers waking up before the sun rose, picking peanuts, pulling weeds, or completing other tasks Dad planned for me in the heat of the day while my peers enjoyed sleeping in or simply being indoors. Many families sought work from my dad; he had a reputation for paying fairly well and often times needed the extra hands to help out on the farm. Though I wasn't afraid of hard work, I couldn't understand why Dad had me in the fields working just as hard as those who sought work from him.

One summer, one answer I sought came as a result of a nosey classmate who worked in Dad's field with her parents, picking peanuts.

"You have Denise working in the field?" she asked Dad.

Dad didn't even flinch when he answered, "I sure do. Denise is no better than anyone else. She has to work just like everyone else. I have her working because she needs to learn that she has to work for a living like others."

I didn't understand at first, but I eventually came to appreciate the work ethic my father instilled inside of me.

Even back then, I never thought I was too good to work in the field, I just didn't want to work there. A while later, after a conversation with a fellow Girl Scout, I wondered if I gave off the impression that I was better than everyone else. It was certainly not how I felt, so I couldn't imagine exuding it, but apparently, I did.

"You know, I never really liked you because I thought you believed you were better than others, but you are actually nice and cool to be around," the girl declared boldly.

Confirmation.

It's amazing the things and experiences we remember. Then and even now I am amazed that I have heard the same sentiments of prejudgment of myself from others. It was my confidence, quiet nature and staying to myself which gave off mixed vibes of who I truly am. That was the discovery I needed to advance to my breakthrough.

Words Don't Hurt...Or do They?

On top of my burn, I was also born with what most called "big eyes". I never thought my eyes were out of the ordinary, until naysayers pointed it out. My eyes - just as my scar, drew names such as *bug eyes* and *fisheyes*. There were times the really creative kids combined the insults into a single disparaging moniker: *bug eyed burn up face*. My peers found any and everything to tease me about, even my smile. *Kool-Aid smile* was the clever name I got for my grin.

I vividly recall one spring, towards the end of 8th grade year, my teacher gave me a strange look. I had no idea what was happening, but I soon found out what had her so worried.

"Oh my! What happened to your face?" she asked loudly. Her booming question caused everyone in the class to gawk at me.

I hated the stares and hated the answer that I had to give to her even more. "This has been here all year," I answered quietly. "It was an accident that happened when I was little."

I was baffled that she never noticed my face until that moment, but was even more perplexed that she asked me in front of the class. It seemed to me that she would be sensitive enough to either pull me aside or at least wait until we were alone to ask. I concluded that some adults are just as insensitive as kids.

The constant stares, name calling, and questioning hammered at my self-esteem. My parents called me beautiful, but no one else saw that, at least I didn't think they did based on the negative comments I kept hearing.

Were my parents lying to me? Did they call me beautiful because I'm their child? I mean, every parent thinks their child is beautiful, right? I couldn't help but wonder what was wrong with me? Did God make me this way so people could make fun of me?

As I got older, I understood that kids will indeed be kids, and sometimes they say and do things without giving much thought to how much it may hurt the other person. But what about adults? Aren't they supposed to know better? Aren't they supposed to do better? I thought so, but I learned that just like kids, sometimes adults can be just as cruel. I heard some of those same names while I was in college too. The stories I could share are chilling.

For example, while I was at work one day, a young man walked up to me.

"Can I ask you a question?" he asked.

I was all set to help this gentleman, so I smiled and answered. "Yes, of course."

He smiled. "How long does it take you to go to sleep?"

I don't know if the confusion I felt on the inside showed on my face or not. That was a weird question, but he was a customer, so I didn't want to be rude and ignore him, or worse, leave him unattended.

So, I indulged him.

"Not long," I answered.

"Oh." He continued staring at me.

"Why do you ask?" Curiosity got the best of me.

"I was wondering because I was thinking it must take you hours to close those big eyes," he laughed hysterically.

I wished I could've ended our conversation before he had the opportunity to degrade me.

I was caught off guard and didn't know how to respond, so I didn't say anything at all. How do you respond to ignorance? I glared at him a moment, transported back to middle school. This guy no longer was the grown man I saw at first. Standing before me was a schoolyard bully just like the ones I'd faced years ago.

I walked away, feelings hurt, but there was no way I was about to let him see that he'd gotten to me. I'd perfected my "brave" face over the years. There are a lot of inconsiderate and ignorant people in this world. Just like the younger version of me, I tucked his insult away, allowing it to fester with all the others. No one knew how many times my feelings were hurt and how those thoughtless names made me feel less than the person I was created to be.

Through the years, I found myself eyeing other women with what I thought were large eyes and asked myself or whomever was with me, "Do my eyes look like hers?" Because when I looked at myself, I did not see eyes as big as a bug's or fish as people taunted. Then there were times when I would look at other women, aware that I was the only person in the room with a scar on her face. It didn't register to me that some of them may have been concealing their facial scar(s) like I was. This prompted me to realize that scars are not always visible; especially emotional ones. How do I know? Because I struggle with both emotional and physical scars.

Eventually the name calling decreased, but the inadequacies I felt remained. I did my best not to let it affect me but often, it did. There were moments when I felt very comfortable with myself. During those times, I didn't care what people thought or said about me. I wasn't sure if my confidence had grown or if the novelty of my look was no longer as unique as it once was. Maybe I'd become so common that my scar was no longer the focus of my bullies or for me.

People cut me deep with their words, but today I can only recall the names I was called way more than I remember the people behind the name calling. That's why I don't agree when people say, "They're just words," or "Words don't hurt." Whenever I hear someone use either term, I immediately know that they've never been on the receiving end of hate.

I can tell you that as bad as those words hurt me, they never broke me. I'm thankful that I never completely lost touch with myself or even caused harm to myself or others, even though I was tempted to.

Hurt people, hurt people.

I never dealt with my hurt by transferring it onto someone else, but I do believe that's what was done to me. Now I understand the children and adults who went above and beyond to hurt me were obviously hurting themselves and my physical features made me an easy target. It took years for me to realize that it wasn't about me. Their own pain was the true culprit in those situations.

Inconsistent Confidence

I t's difficult to explain how I had confidence in myself, yet struggled with self-assurance. My parents did a fantastic job of instilling an attitude in me that sparked my confidence outwardly, but experience drowned that same confidence from the inside.

While many think confidence and security are one in the same, they are different. I was independent and exuded confidence, despite lacking self-esteem and accepting my scars. I wasn't as collected as people thought I was. I held back my feelings, dealing with people in a manner that would keep me from being disappointed. That's when my insecurity level soared off the charts.

I don't recall when my self-esteem plummeted. It began as a result of a string of failed relationships, with friends, family, and other tumultuous encounters throughout my life. Those painful experiences shattered and left me in broken pieces.

This quiet, yet outgoing kid grew up in an undeveloped small city in the south, Sumter, South Carolina, with a population of roughly 10,000 people. Growing up, my parents kept me involved in several activities that helped shape and mold me. I took ballet, tap, and jazz dance classes, piano lessons, sang in my church choir, was a member of the Girls Scouts as well as 4-H, and I participated and won several pageants. Yes – pageants: debutant, cotillion, church, and state. There were several pageants where I had to present myself in a fashionable manner while speaking and exhibiting a talent. While those pageants were not considered beauty pageants, each required a level of confidence and the desire to do your best. It took a lot to stand in front of a crowd just as it's taking a lot for me to pour my life and emotions into this book.

After I grew up and moved away, South Carolina was still the place where I felt safe and free. I didn't realize how much of my hometown confidence had dwindled away until I ran into a high school classmate in Walmart while visiting home. We chatted for a while, and before parting ways, he asked if we could take a picture. I loved taking pictures, but this particular one made me nervous.

I wasn't wearing makeup because I was home and didn't feel the need to cover up. I immediately felt anxious. I had no clue who would see the picture once he tagged me on Facebook, which I had no doubt he'd do. I agreed to take the picture and did what I always did: position myself to the right, so the "good" side of my face would show.

My "right" side was literally the right side of my body; my scar is on the left side of my face. I tilted my head, positioned just right for the scar not to show and smiled for the selfie. My classmate had no idea the person in that picture wasn't Denise from South Carolina who was carefree and outgoing. I was Denise who moved near the District of Columbia and succumbed to the superficial "city life," where in order to fit in, you had to appear to be perfect. Perfection - in my mind, meant no scars. At least none anyone could see.

Not Sent for Me

From elementary through high school, there was nothing I could do to hide my scar. I didn't wear makeup; hadn't even realized it was an option. In college, I got more creative with my hairstyles. I wore my hair to the side, allowing it to hang over my scar. I hadn't dated a lot of guys in high school or college; the relationships that I did have back then all ended at some point. I often wondered if my scar played a role in the demise of those relationships. I knew some men were superficial, and more concerned with external beauty than the inside of women. Knowing this led me to conclude that my scar was indeed the cause of my nonexistent love life.

One evening when I was in college, I saw this guy on campus who I had a slight crush on. We had spoken a few times in person and on the phone, but that evening outside our dorms, I guess he really saw me for the first time.

"What happened to your face?" he asked.

Unlike my past experiences where that same question made me feel bad, I'd grown to appreciate people asking instead of staring. I opened up and told him about the childhood accident. I never saw or heard from him after that night. My feelings were hurt. Without another conversation, I was left to believe that he lost interest because he couldn't see past my scar.

27

My spirit was a bit bruised, but that didn't stop me from opening myself up to the possibility of a real relationship. I met other guys who seemed genuine in the beginning and led me to believe that we were exclusive, but I would later find out that wasn't the case.

Some of those same guys who disappeared on me, reached out in later years. I was open to their apologies for being less than mature during our courtship; however, I wasn't open to rekindling the flames I'd extinguished long ago. Getting over them was the easy part; getting over the thought that my scar caused our relationship to fail, wasn't so easy.

During some of my conversations with these former and/or potential boyfriends, I worked up the courage to ask if they treated me the way they did because of my scar. Each one told me my scar had nothing to do with their behavior. In fact, the common response to the reasoning for the problems back then was their own lack of maturity. One guy said, "Losing you was the worst mistake in my life." I whole heartedly accepted the apologies and wished them well. Their answers caused me to do a self-assessment and I found that once again, I assumed the worst. I blamed my scar for those failed relationships, when all along it was their deficiency.

Have you ever found yourself in a similar situation? Maybe yours weren't physical scars. Maybe it was weight or height or something else that you viewed as a hindrance in your life. You've probably spent years, like I did, blaming yourself when it may have had nothing to do with you at all. Maybe now is a good time to consider that true love sees beyond the flaws. Let go of the guilt and gain a new perspective. If it didn't work out, it had nothing to do with your physical appearance and everything to do with the mentality of the other person. I know from experience that the right person won't look at you and see your scar; they'll only see you. That's the person you want in your life.

When I began writing this book, I admit I did not allow myself to get close enough to others to form impactful relationships. As I have reassessed myself and those that rely on me in various manners, I realize that there are a lot of people who seem to need me despite my attempts to keep them at a distance. There are many people who trust me and rely on me to provide positive feedback about things going on in their lives. I've often tried to hold back, fearful that I may not be all they think I am, that I may not fit in with them if they knew I looked different under my concealer or if they knew the emotional baggage behind my *Kool-Aid* smile.

As early as elementary school, I learned how to harden my attitude and became disenfranchised with having friends, but it wasn't until my senior year of high school that I truly mastered it. In high school, it wasn't uncommon to have girls pretending to be my friends one day, then start a **Don't talk to Denise** campaign the next. I can't count the number of hours I spent worried over how to make these relationships better. One day, I was fed up and couldn't keep pretending the actions of those so-called friends didn't bother me. I had to say something.

"I'm tired of the back and forth. Either we're friends or we're not. I'm okay either way," I said.

I was no longer going to give them the satisfaction of thinking they'd gotten to me. Even though I knew girls will be girls, I still couldn't stop the questions flooding my brain.

What caused these issues to begin with? Was it because of my scar or were they that immature and mean?

I looked forward to leaving high school behind and the emotional rollercoaster that came with it. I couldn't wait to get to college so I could engage in new, more mature friendships and experiences and be around people on another level than all those childish high schoolers.

At least, that's what I was hoping.

Unfortunately, college didn't bring many new experiences in the friend category. I had girls that I hung out with and really enjoyed being around. In fact, I thought we were really building bonds that would last forever. A few events happened which changed my thoughts, however.

One night, it became evident that my purpose in the group wasn't about friendship, it was about my car; or so events would lead me to believe. I was the only friend in the group with transportation, so being nice to me was beneficial.

On this particular day I received what I'll call the worst invite ever. I stopped by to visit two of my friends. As we sat and talked, one of them said, "So, we were thinking about going to this party later on, but we're not sure how we're going to get there."

"Hey, how about you come too, Denise?" The other girl recited from their perfectly planned skit.

I'm not sure how they expected me to respond to that invite, but I'm sure they didn't receive the answer they were hoping to get. It was clear to me that I wasn't invited because they wanted me there or because we were all such good friends that they wanted to spend time with me. No, they needed a ride. I had no doubt that if they didn't think it would've sound too ridiculous, they probably would've asked to borrow my car and left me out altogether.

That experience left me, once again, questioning myself.

Was I not good enough?

Was I not pretty enough?

What made them see me only as a reliable ride, but not a friend?

What hurt more than anything was that one of these ladies and I were once inseparable. But that situation - along with others, put a strain on our friendship. I missed what we had, but I wasn't mature enough to express how she hurt my feelings. By this time, I'd perfected the art of holding my hurt emotions inside, so that's what I chose to do.

Count on Me

During my time in college, I lived on campus but traveled home most weekends to work or do other things. At the time I couldn't see what I was doing, but going home so often was my way of shielding myself from potential hurts. If I would've remained on campus too much, I ran the risk of fostering more relationships that would most likely end with me being hurt. In hindsight, I wish I allowed myself more time on campus to just live and be free, but I guess I wasn't quite ready for that life. In fact, at some point I lost focus and felt my life spiraling down a path I did not want to take. I took a break from school and joined the United States Air National Guard. I went through Basic Training and Technical School. Upon completion, I returned home more focused and determined to complete my degree and graduate.

After graduating from college, I packed up my life and moved to Richmond, Virginia. It was there that I fulfilled my desire of becoming a member of Delta Sigma Theta Sorority, Incorporated. It's one of the largest sororities, with more than 300,000 members and there were 59 other women initiated with me in 1996. I was surrounded by all those women, yet I often felt alone. Imagine that.

Our chosen song for our bond was "Count on Me," by Whitney Houston and CeCe Winans. During our gatherings, I could not help but wonder if I truly fit in. I never shared those thoughts with anyone, nor have I ever thrown public pity parties. Those parties were always held in isolation. Besides in my mind, no one wanted to hear how I felt, or maybe I'd suppressed my feelings for so long, I never learned how to share them.

Experience Meets Maturity

While living in Richmond, I received a job offer which transferred me to Alexandria, Virginia. It was there that I was met with the true test of fitting in.

The area - known as the DMV, representing the District of Columbia, Maryland, and Virginia, introduced me to a life of luxuries this girl with a scar from the south was not quite ready for. Not only was I trying to fit in, but I was 23 years old, on my own and further away from my family. Creating a roadmap for myself was not easy, but I did it.

On one of my trips back to South Carolina, I was invited to an event. I accepted the invitation and everything was going well.

Until it happened.

While speaking with a few acquaintances, I noticed a guy staring at me. It was apparent he had something on his mind. He walked up to me and what he did next left me speechless and appalled. I was still wearing my hair in a style that hid my scar. So, when he approached me, he said, "I've seen you before."

"No, I don't think so," I replied.

He reached out, moved my hair to the side, then nodded. "Yeah, I have seen you before."

I stood in shock, especially since I didn't know him. I don't think he really knew me either, but he definitely knew my scar. All I could think was how tacky and rude he was and that my scar had apparently become a form of identification. I never wanted anyone to avoid me because of my scar, but I certainly didn't want to be known because of it.

That incident was the final straw.

When I returned north, I sought cosmetic consultation. My childhood doctor in Port Chester, New York advised once I was older, I could have a skin grafting procedure. Well, I was at the point where I wanted to see what the process entailed and prayed it would remove the scar which had controlled my life for too many years.

During my consultation, the doctor had the most bizarre observation. "You have the perfect scar," he stated.

I was confused. I would use a lot of words to describe my scar, but perfect wasn't one of them.

"How's it perfect?" I asked.

He smiled, amused by my question. Of course, I wouldn't see my scar as perfect, that's why I was there in the first place. Being a professional, he was able to see what I couldn't.

"It's not raised with a keloid so I wouldn't have to cut it down and smooth it out. It's also not indented so I wouldn't need to fill it. It's just darker than the rest of your face. Hyperpigmentation is the reason it's so noticeable."

I nodded as he explained my "perfect" scar. Everything sounded promising until he hit me with the bad news.

"If we do any type of procedure, it would most likely make the scar or the area of skin around it worse."

My heart dropped. I came to him so he could help me and make the scar go away or at least make it less noticeable. I didn't want to exacerbate the situation. I didn't need time to think about my decision.

I left the scar alone.

After my disappointing doctor's visit, I discovered all hope was not gone. I learned about microdermabrasion treatments. These treatments used a machine which rubbed back and forth on my scar to remove layers of skin. The goal was to lighten the scar and make it less noticeable. After my treatments, I incorporated a prescribed cream into my skin care regimen, which peeled my skin. Initially, the skin came off in thin film-like pieces. On one occasion, I attempted to assist with the peeling process by removing some of it myself. Evidentially, I removed too much skin, because the pink flesh underneath peeked through.

"What have I done?" I screamed at my horrified reflection in the mirror. I made it worse! There was no way I'd be able to hide it. I successfully managed to do the one thing I didn't want to do… brought more attention to my scar.

It wasn't until years later, after conducting more research about dermabrasions, that I learned that the procedure wasn't likely to work with my skin color or my type of scar. The only thing I accomplished was giving money to a company that wasn't designed for me. I should have accepted the report of the doctor who told me my scar was perfect and left well enough alone.

Magical Solution

Immediately after making my scar worse, I researched ways to camouflage my mistake. This brought me to what I view as a God send. I came across a brand of makeup used specifically for concealing scars and it changed my life. Up until that point I'd never thought about using makeup to cover my blemish. I rushed out and found my God send to see what miracle could happen.

All I could do was pray that I'd found the answer I'd been seeking for so long.

I made it home from the store, and immediately applied the concealer. I couldn't believe it! Just like that, my scar was gone. Not totally gone, but enough to fade it. I couldn't stop looking at myself. It worked wonders. After a successful public appearance following my first use, I was addicted to it.

I needed that concealer as bad as I needed air. It was my lifeline. Without it I felt vulnerable and naked, but wearing it gave me a sense of confidence I never imagined I could possess. I felt like I'd stepped into a whole new world. A world where people would see me and only me. A world where no one would stare at my face and question me about my scar. A world where my hair could be styled any way I wanted, and I didn't have to use it as a shield. I loved all the possibilities this new world brought me.

I was so excited about my new discovery, I didn't see how I'd freed myself from one problem only to become hostage to another. The freedom I so desperately wanted to experience never came. Once again, I'd created a crutch. Something else to depend on. Another cover hiding the real me. Even though reality sounded an alarm inside of me, I pressed mute and kept going. The makeup was a cover, but the alternative was a destination I didn't want to revisit.

After years of being teased about them, people finally noticed my eyes and smile in a different way. The facial features which were once the center of jokes, had become my most complimented assets. I longed to hear those compliments for so many years, but by the time they came, it was too late. I couldn't receive compliments without wondering if those people would've seen my beautiful eyes and bright smile if my scar wasn't hidden behind my concealer. Even though I questioned the compliments, I enjoyed hearing them a lot more than the ridicule. The lack of attention due to my scar had become such a wonderful feeling. So much so, that the thought of showing my scar to anyone was frightening. Especially those who'd never seen it before. I didn't want to go back to feeling different, or questioning people's motives in my life.

Today, I'm in a new frame of mind. I'm tired of hiding behind hair and concealer. I am who I am, and I've made up my mind that the people who love and care for me will still love and care for me, scar and all.

I wrote this book not only for myself and others, but it also serves as a big reveal. There were people in my life who still didn't know about my scar even while I was writing. Once I decided to tell my story, I discovered courage I didn't know I possessed. The courage that would allow people to learn about my emotional and physical scars and the apprehensions that had lived inside of me for years.

****

I must be totally honest and admit that I don't plan on getting rid of my concealer. However, I'll only wear it when I want to and on days when I don't feel like wearing it, I won't. I'll go out unapologetically. The accident didn't happen to me by chance. It didn't take God by surprise. For some reason I was chosen to bear this scar.

I've spent years hiding my shame instead of walking in my purpose. I believe God was waiting for me to get to the point where I could confidently stand up, embrace, and manage my imperfection with style and grace. It took years for me to understand that my parents nor I had control over what God planned to happen to me on that cold day in February 1973.

My Reasons are Different

Women wear makeup for various reasons. I have often wondered how many women I've interacted with daily were hiding physical scars. How many were like me, hiding behind concealers and thick makeup? My curiosity led me to do some research and that research - although very brief, revealed some interesting information about some of my favorite onscreen celebrities. I was surprised to find out that some of them have scars which aren't visible. The thought of being a celebrity on television and movie screens with a scar seemed impossible to me. From the outside looking in, those celebrities didn't allow their scars to keep them down.

Before I discovered the concealer, all I wanted was for people to give me a chance to show them I'm not the monster or side show they made me feel like with their stares. After I discovered the concealer, I became very comfortable remaining silent about what was behind it.

I loved how my now invisible scar helped people look me in my eyes when speaking to me instead of gawking at the side of my face. It's like how I imagine women with large breasts feel with people leering at their bosom during the conversation, rather than the woman – reducing them to objects rather than a human.

Finding My Mate

I quickly learned that hiding behind concealer was not going to help me find a mate, which turned out to be an emotional rollercoaster. I never liked rollercoasters, and I disliked the rides men took me on even more. I had to admit that not all of my relationships ended dreadfully. Some of them were funny and light natured, while others were devastating.

One guy I met after I started wearing concealer really hurt me. We had a brief, yet wonderful conversation and exchanged numbers. After conversing several times, we went on a dinner date. I made a point to tell him about my scar before we continued courting, because I felt as if a part of me was hiding something major. Besides, things were going so well, I was ready to let my guard down.

After dinner, I disclosed my secret.

"I had a great time," I said. "We seem to hit it off really well."

"I feel the same way, I look forward to many more dinners," he smiled.

"I want to share something with you," I told him, feeling comfortable.

"Sure, what's on your mind?"

"When I was six months old, I fell on a radiator and was burned on my left cheek." I turned to show him the area and followed up with, "You can't really see it because I have on a little makeup but I wanted to let you know so it wouldn't be awkward if you saw it."

"I can barely see it," he replied, eyeing me as if he was trying to see the scar for himself. "Thank you for telling me."

We chatted more about the accident and my scar, and he made me feel like it was no big deal.

The next day, I called and left a message to thank him for a great evening. Several days passed and he hadn't responded, which was unusual. I called again and left another message. Weeks later, he left me a message saying he met someone else and wanted to see where things could go with her. I wasn't crushed, but I was blindsided. It seemed like things were going great before he knew about my scar. It could've been a coincidence things played out the way they did, but in my mind...my announcement was the culprit.

I understand that I can't control other people - all I can do is control my reaction to them. I do believe, however, that my reaction commands maturity that leads to understanding.

I met my concealer before I met the man who'd eventually become my husband. Every time he saw me, I was well covered. I thought I was in a pretty good space in my life by the time I met him, but I was still leading a double life. While I was very poised on the outside, I carried a lack of confidence internally. I had the ability to be as great as everyone expected me to be if I had my magical concealer.

When my husband and I met, I was in graduate school, living on my own. I was single, and happy about it or at least accepting it. I wasn't looking for love, which is exactly when love happens.

We lived over an hour away from each other, which gave us a chance to do a lot of talking and in the process, we created a strong bond and a genuine friendship. Of course, in the back of my mind, I was thinking about the big reveal. The more I got to know him, the more comfortable I felt. Eventually, he made it known that he desired more face time with me.

His words, though very sweet, made me very nervous. I knew our relationship couldn't continue the way it was going, being that we hardly saw each other. Of course, the time was going to come when we would want to spend more time in each other's presence, but I couldn't stop thinking the worst. I wasn't ready to endure another failed relationship. Wasn't ready to start second guessing myself once again. All of that was scary, but there was something else on my mind that was even scarier.

I didn't want our relationship to become more serious than it was without him knowing about my scar. The more time passed, the more I pondered my dilemma. Time continued passing and I knew I couldn't put it off any longer. It was time to be open about my scar.

I wasn't nervous about sharing my scar with him. I didn't know which way things would go, but I was prepared in case he dumped me after my reveal. I reminded myself that failed relationships weren't new to me. I'd been down that road before and each time I came out a better version of me than I was before. If it happened again, I'd use it for my good. That's what my head said. I wasn't sure if my heart was on the same page, but I was really hoping it received the message. The last thing I wanted to do was spend time mending another broken heart.

This conversation was too intimate for public discussion, so I arranged date night at my home. The details I was about to share weren't for a crowded restaurant or in a quiet movie theater.

"I need to tell you something that could change your mind about me," I told him right after we greeted each other. I had to get it out while I had the nerve. I saw the curiosity in his eyes, so I didn't make him wait.

I recounted the accident, with him hanging onto every word. As I disclosed the experiences I'd dealt with throughout my life as a result of the scar, he sat motionless. His expression was difficult to read, but I did see a tinge of sadness in his eyes. Once I ran out of words, I excused myself for a moment. I needed him to see me…all of me.

So, I went to the bathroom and removed the concealer.

I reached the point of no return. Taking a deep breath, I stepped back into the room, nervous to see what direction our relationship was about to take. When he noticed me, he stood up and waited for me to stop. I didn't walk all the way up to him, but I was close enough for him to see. Time froze as I waited for him to say something. Anything.

He closed the gap between us, leaned down and gently kissed my scar. "Is this what you're worried about?" he asked.

I nodded.

"You are still beautiful," he said.

We talked more and from that moment on we became inseparable. He made me feel comfortable being myself. So much so, that I contemplated going in public without my concealer. That thought only lasted a moment because not long after that day, I allowed his friends - unbeknownst to them, to change my mind.

When I think about it, I was again protecting someone from enduring any pain stemming from me. I never shared with him how I felt about allowing his friends to see or even know about my scar. In hindsight, a simple conversation could've ended my uncertainty of how to interact with them. I could've released my insecurities and allowed him to help me tackle them. I don't think it ever dawned on him that my scar anxiety didn't end with him. I carried it to each new acquaintance, and his friends were no exception. Maybe I would've felt a little better if I didn't already know so much about his past relationships.

I appreciated him being transparent with me, but I did not expect his past to intimidate me the way it did. He dated women who were considered to be "show-pieces", women who could've very well have been models had they not chosen other paths. Most of the women he described (some I saw through photos), were quite different from me. These women were lighter, taller, had long hair, and none of them had facial blemishes.

All of this played in my head the day I was about to meet some of his best friends. I was nervous as heck. How were they going to view me in comparison to the women they were used to seeing him date? There was no way I was going to meet them without my concealer. I felt like I already had enough stacked against me, I didn't need to add my scar to the list. Not only that, I didn't want to embarrass my man in front of his friends; I was already working hard to meet the standard of the women he previously dated.

We had a great relationship and an even better friendship, which meant there was nothing I couldn't tell him, and he wouldn't understand. Knowing all of this, I should've told him about my anxiety and my feelings about meeting his friends. Instead, I kept it to myself, met his friends, then later asked what his friends had to say about me. He was honest, another quality I loved about him.

"One of my friends said you don't look like my normal type," he informed me.

"What does that mean?" I knew exactly what he meant, but for some reason I needed to hear him say it.

"You know, like I told you, most of my girlfriends have been light-skinned model types. That's just who they're accustomed to seeing me with."

"Was there anything else?" I asked.

He thought for a moment. "Well, yeah."

"Tell me," I insisted.

"Another friend did ask if I was sure I wanted to get serious with you and leave the other women I normally date alone."

I didn't know how I was supposed to respond after hearing that. A part of me wished I never asked. I understood that they were his friends long before we met; they kept it real with him. They probably didn't expect him to tell me, but that's the relationship he and I created. We believed in sharing the truth.

I guess my silence rang loudly in his ear because he felt the need to explain. "I promise you they weren't saying those things to be negative towards you. They just know I had a certain type and they didn't want me to lead you on if I'm not serious. Their intentions were good, I promise."

I accepted his words and his assurance, then I did what I did best. I internalized my feelings and made sure my issues didn't make him feel uncomfortable. Over time, I pushed his friends' concerns out of my mind. At least I thought I did until they planned a group outing, which I should've expected sooner or later. They wanted all of us to meet up with their wives, which was scary. If the men had opinions, I could only imagine what the women would say.

There was no need trying to avoid it, so I agreed to go with him. Upon meeting the wives, I immediately identified one trait he and his friends had in common: they were attracted to the same type of women. I was among all of these beautiful ladies, trying hard to hide my scars and my anxieties.

When his friends asked if he was sure about dating me, the answer was yes. Almost 20 years of marriage proved that we were both sure. Many of the wives and girlfriends I met that night are no longer around today for one reason or another. While we've certainly experienced our share of challenges throughout the years, there's one thing that hasn't changed...his support. He's remained by my side and encouraged me along the way. He's made it a point to make sure I know how beautiful I am to him.

His only wish is for me to see what he sees in me.

Breaking Point

Concealing my scar wasn't reserved just for being away from home; I covered up at the house, too - especially if we had guests over. Even my sons' friends.

I either wore the concealer, or avoided whomever was visiting the house. Yes - I hid from kids, too. It's that simple; anxiety doesn't discriminate. I feared the children would look at me differently, but my biggest concern was them questioning my children about my face, or worse...teasing them about it. I wanted to protect my sons from being tormented because of me.

My sons never came close to being teased, but as their mother and protector I had to be cautious. I prayed for the best, but stayed guarded for the worst. Fear causes me to be preemptive, hoping to make life better for others - especially those I hold near to my heart.

My children and husband have no idea the lengths I've gone through to protect them, or at least my idea of protecting them. My children are unaware that when their friends stayed overnight, I did everything I needed to do before going to bed so I wouldn't have to come back out. Once I cleaned my face, I disappeared for the rest of the night. The boys probably wouldn't understand why I dabbed on concealer in the morning before leaving my room to avoid their friends seeing my bare face, but I did what I had to do. Home should've been the one place where I felt comfortable being myself.

It wasn't.

My unhealthy attachment to my concealer became evident one evening when my son and his friend asked to go to the movies. I purchased their tickets online, and picked up his friend on the way. I thought about putting on my concealer, but since it was a late movie and I didn't need to go inside the theater, I didn't bother.

What a huge mistake.

We arrived at the theater and I dropped the boys off at the door, waiting for them to enter safely before driving away. Moments later, my cell phone rang. It was my son calling; the reason triggered my anxiety.

"Mom, the staff said they need an adult to walk us in the movie."

I was so uncomfortable with the thought of getting out of that car, I was paralyzed. What if I saw someone I knew? What if people stared? What if my son's friend saw me? Really, saw me?

I drove in circles, searching for a parking spot while planning a swift entry and exit strategy without being seen. I pulled over to an illegal parking area, just to gather and deliver myself a much-needed pep talk. I calmed down, convincing myself I had to behave like the adult that I was and needed to focus on helping my son and his friend, which was all that mattered.

I parked in the garage and bravely walked into the theatre, with my youngest son in tow.

Of course, even after my pep talk, entering the building wasn't an easy feat. I was careful not to turn my head in a manner that would disclose my scar, virtually performing theatrics to accomplish my goal and get back to the safety of my car. Success! But once I made it back to my car, I realized I forgot to get my ticket validated. I thought about going back in, but that was not about to happen. I made it out safely and would rather pay the fee than risk going back inside.

Back at home, I reflected on what happened, wondering if I had a panic attack. My behavior was unhealthy, and I needed to get to the bottom of it. I was putting a tremendous amount of stress on myself and it made me ill. My husband wasn't home at the time, and I didn't have friends to call - at least not about what happened, because no one knew how deep my feelings were about myself and my scars.

The more I thought about it, I saw how out of control my feelings were. It was uncomfortable knowing that I continually hid behind a disguise. My unconventional way of life was beginning to weigh heavily on me; it was crucial to do something about it. I asked God for strength to get over my anxieties and grant me the confidence to walk without fear. That night, I decided a change needed to be made. I officially declared I would confess to everyone about my scar.

I would heal by sharing my testimony through my writing.

Checking Myself Out

At the beginning of 2019 before recognizing how I was mentally damaging myself; I sought a different approach to treating the Premenstrual Tension Syndrome I suffered from.

Instead of making an appointment with my regular physician, I visited a Holistic Integrative Medicine Center. This health agency boasted Naturopathic Physicians who focused on identifying the root of health issues rather than treating the symptoms presented by the patient.

After checking in, I sat reading information about the doctor I was scheduled to see. The pamphlet detailed the doctor's training and certifications, which put me at ease. Additionally, it noted her education and appointments to advisory boards; there was even a picture of the doctor - a young, petite, black woman. Out of all the information the clinic provided about the doctor, there was one detail omitted from her bio that wasn't visible in her photo.

"Good morning Denise, are you ready? Come on back." The doctor appeared when I wasn't paying attention, startling me.

"Good morning," I responded. "Lead the way."

As we walked back to her office, the doctor asked, "How are you feeling?"

"I'm doing well," I anxiously replied. I had already taken a hormonal test three weeks prior, and was excited to receive the results. I was working out more and changing my eating habits, both which seemed to aid in soothing my ailments.

"I have your results from the hormonal exam and would like to review them with you," the doctor advised. "Have you ever heard of cortisol?"

"No ma'am," I answered hesitantly, unsure of what she was about to share.

"Cortisol is a hormone that is released from your adrenal glands into your body when you are stressed. Your body does not produce enough cortisol to kick in to help you when you're stressed. What are some things that are causing you stress?"

Instead of responding I froze, noticing her hands for the first time. I'd seen them before, but now they stood out.

I pondered the situations that were causing me stress - warranted or not. Work, hiding my scars (emotional and physical), trying to appear to be perfect. I suddenly saw how the doctor and I both had visible scars in common.

As she took notes, I was in awe of the discolored patches of skin covering the doctor's hands. The discoloration wasn't anywhere else I could see, but it was obvious that she suffered from vitiligo. I could have been wrong, because as most people did with me, I assumed. The difference was, I didn't stare.

I couldn't bring myself to tell the doctor how I freaked out over concealer every day. It sounded insane to admit out loud. I wasn't able to express how I wondered day in and day out who saw past the self-confident smokescreen I put up, or about the various excursions I missed out on because I feared my scar would show. I couldn't tell her I wasn't completely being myself, and had bottled all of these feelings inside for years. I couldn't freely vent to her, and that's exactly how I felt with everyone else.

Who wanted to hear about my struggles?

In hindsight, I could have benefited from asking the doctor about her condition and how she handles it. But I would not have been able to afford that discussion, since insurance didn't cover this visit. Instead, I kept my answer simple.

"Between the commute to and from work, projects, and balancing life at home, I have a few stressful things on my plate."

Seeing the lost pigmentation on her hands and possibly other places on her body, made the greatest burden of my life seem so small; I didn't want to complain. The doctor's hands served as reminders of people who try to compare the scars on their legs, back, chest, and areas on their body that can be concealed with clothing to mine. When they attempt to encourage me with stories about their scars which are anywhere other than their face, it's hard for me to receive.

I often wonder what my life would have been like had that radiator burned my leg, back, or arm - anywhere but my face. The doctor's disfigured hands were equal to my face. Unless she wore gloves, there was no way to hide them.

Not even makeup would work.

My appointment ended with the doctor explaining how more exercise, rest, and stress reduction were the best remedies for my health concerns. Additionally, she recommended naturopathic medicines to provide adrenal support to my body.

Prior to this meeting, I never heard of cortisol or how it aids the body with dealing with stress. I knew I stressed out from time to time, but there were never any incidents that caused me to feel totally overwhelmed. At least that's what I thought. I couldn't think of any issues I was dealing with that made me stress unknowingly.

…not once had I considered the day to day concealing and emotional scars within.

My Chapter 47

By August of 2019, I formulated the idea of this book. As I prepared to celebrate getting closer to exiting my 40s and entering chapter 47, my world was rocked by a couple of surprises that stirred up deeply buried emotions. It was a birthday like none other, impacting me in ways I never imagined. You never know how a few simple words can make a difference in a person's life.

I'm often described as loyal, genuine, humorous, and confident. Out of those descriptions, self-confidence is the one I struggled with from time to time. On my 47th birthday, I brought my smile and donuts to work. It was my special day, and I wanted others to feel the same joy I felt on my day. In between meetings, I socialized with a few co-workers, sharing my plans for the evening.

After work, my husband took me to dinner to Claudia's, in downtown D.C. I was immediately impressed with the ambience. The sound of joyful chatter and utensils clanking against plates could be heard as we made our way to our table. I couldn't stop a smile from taking over my face when I spotted a champagne bucket sitting in the middle of our black glass table. I figured my husband must've made the restaurant staff aware of my birthday, and requested this setup.

Not long after we were seated, my husband excused himself to go to the restroom. While he was away, I continued admiring the champagne bucket and its contents. I decided to capture this special moment he created, so I took a few photos. As I took the last photo, I saw a card leaning against the bucket.

Wishing you a magical evening. Happy Birthday Denise!

I was stunned to find the name on the card wasn't my husband's; this wasn't his idea. I was still focused on the card when a waiter came to the table.

"Your friend called," he said. "She wanted to make sure you had a great birthday, so she ordered this for you." He smiled and nodded towards the champagne.

My heart felt all the love through her words and actions. I couldn't wait to call and say thank you. My eyes filled with tears.

S*he listened to me, she heard me, and she cares about me.*

Earlier, I shared my dinner plans with my colleague, who'd recently become a very good friend. She and I had known each other a few years, but we never really talked about life outside of work. About a month or two before my birthday, she approached me for advice on a personal matter. I could tell that she needed someone who would listen and really hear what she had to say. I was overjoyed that she saw something in me that made her feel comfortable enough to come to me. I understood what she was feeling; I often felt the same way, but even after helping her through her problems, I kept mine to myself. My problems were my responsibility, not hers. Besides, she didn't want to hear all of that.

At least that's what I told myself.

The next week, I was still floating from my amazing birthday celebration, and thought all the surprises were over, but I was wrong. I received an invitation to lunch from another colleague, who like the previous colleague, was also a friend. At lunch, she presented me with a birthday card.

"This lunch is to celebrate you and your birthday," she said before I opened the card she handed me. Inside, was an original poem she wrote just for me.

You are a beautiful amazing woman.

That was the first line of the poem. Once again, my eyes started sweating. S*he's talking about me,* I thought. *She's calling me amazing and beautiful.*

She had no idea how her words touched me. I continued reading the poem, but what stuck with me was:

You may never know how much you blessed and *not once have you judged or shamed.*

All I did was provide a listening ear to both ladies. I gave them what I wanted for myself, but wouldn't allow myself to openly talk with them the way they'd opened up to me. It wasn't that I didn't trust them. There was something on the inside, blocking me from releasing my hurt and pain to anyone. I remained available when needed, but never shed my protective shield or dealt with my shortcomings. It never occurred to me how my story could've helped them just as much as it should have helped me.

New Mind Set

I entered 2020 with a made-up mind.

I continued unpacking all my junk, while acknowledging I'm not perfect and basking in the glory of imperfection the Lord has blessed me with. I've received fantastic opportunities in my life, as well as the lives of others. I'm walking in a new light and taking on the challenge of truly setting myself free from thoughts which don't speak positivity into my life or others around me. I know how life works sometimes. Just when you decide to make a change in the right direction, tests appear from nowhere to throw you off course. Even if that happened, I'd remain steadfast and have faith, trusting that greatness in various forms awaits me and everyone I love.

Writing this memoir has awakened me to things I never realized I was doing. Like being held captive by the feelings I wouldn't release, blocking my progress. While I'd experienced some traumatic events and hurtful situations in my earlier years, now I understand that I processed it all wrong. I believed those circumstances arose to tear me down, but I couldn't see how each stone thrown at me actually built me up. The harmful things people did and the names they called me worked together to form the woman I was always meant to be.

I promised myself that 2020 would be the year I'd make new connections, sustain existing connections, and let go of false connections. I would move past my negative outlook, face my fears, and deal with anything that makes me feel substandard.

When I started this book, I acknowledged that I didn't allow myself to get close enough to others to form impactful relationships. As I have reassessed myself and those that rely on me in various ways, I've come to see there are plenty of people who genuinely like me, but aren't aware of the scars I worked so hard to hide. So operation "ConcealHER No More," was in full effect. Well, somewhat… since I decided it would be best for me to take baby steps as I extended myself to others.

I took a deep breath and did something I never imagined I'd ever do.

Compliments Now Accepted

I never saw myself as a victim, but one day I realized that I made myself one by being silent. I moved through life over 40 years without addressing important issues or questions surrounding my experiences and how they made me feel. I have numerous stories showing how inconsiderate people can be. Sometimes it's intentional and sometimes not; clearly without conversations the unknown will remain just that, unknown.

There are those who may feel elevated or inspired when someone calls them beautiful, but it's different for me. When someone calls me beautiful, my first response or thought is to question it. There have been times when I've asked the person to repeat themselves, so I'm clear they're addressing me, and they're certain they meant to say those words to me. Even if their intentions were clear, I still questioned the compliment.

Something must be wrong with them or *they must want or need something from me.*

In my mind, it's always the latter.

I believed most of the time, those people came with hidden agendas.

A great example of this was one day when a homeless man asked me for some change.

"I'm sorry I don't have any money on me," I informed him politely.

He looked at me and smiled. "You are beautiful, can I marry you?"

See? A hidden agenda!

How could he ask me for something first, then proceed to tell me I'm beautiful? I understood the motive behind his compliment. He probably figured if he offered a compliment, I'd find the change he'd requested. Some women would probably say thank you without another thought, but that's not how my brain processed compliments.

Another time, I was shopping at a local store. The woman standing at the door to check my receipt as I walked out said, "You are very pretty."

"Thank you," I responded with an uneasy smile. Sensing my discomfort, the woman followed up with, "No, you are really beautiful. Tell your husband he's a lucky man to have such a beautiful woman."

I forced myself to receive her compliment with sincerity and walked away, wondering if she would think the same if my scar wasn't covered in concealer.

After enduring years of name calling - sometimes even now, those names have a way of resurfacing and making me feel uncomfortable. The difference between now and then? Now I don't claim the names I was called in the past. I was nearing the end of my 40s, and the innocent, hurt little girl inside of me resurfaced some days. I can't pretend I blocked it out. However, I learned that I was bigger than what tried to tear me down. I was committed to holding my head high and proudly accepting compliments as they came my way.

Hard to Turn Around

It pains me to think of how I passed up innumerable opportunities to free myself from my concealer. So often, I could've taken matters in my own hands and lived a life which didn't bind me to my concealer. Everything happens in its own perfect timing, but I still cringed, thinking about those missed opportunities to break free.

After my husband proposed, I hoped I would automatically transition to a comfortable place which allowed me to drop the concealer and not worry about his friends, or anyone else. I wanted to be satisfied knowing that in his eyes, I was good enough. Though I knew that was true in my heart, my mind wouldn't release me.

My next missed opportunity was when I began my career with the Federal Government.

If I had to do it all over again, I would've arrived the first day with my face fully exposed.

I would've welcomed any and all questions about my scar and moved on from there. Instead, I stayed hidden. But there was one person who managed to tear down my walls. In the first few months after I started work, we became fast friends. One day, she visited with me at my home. During the visit, I disclosed my scar showing her pictures of me without the concealer.

She narrowed her eyes, moved the picture closer, then looked at me. "I know you aren't trying to show me a scar on your face in a photo," she said.

"Can't you see it?" I asked, pointing to my face on the picture.

She shook her head. "Not really." She continued staring but still couldn't see it.

I placed the photo on the sofa and said, "I'll be right back."

I left her there while I prepared to once again, wash my face and show someone else my scar. I walked back in the room and stood in front of her.

"That's it?" she asked, pointing to my face.

I nodded with relief, gathering that my scar wasn't a big deal to her. We talked more and she was empathetic to my feelings, but assured me that the scar wasn't as obvious to everyone else as it was to me. We chatted some more and that was the last she and I ever spoke about it.

That was almost 20 years ago.

My friend had probably forgotten our talk until I gave birth to my oldest son. She visited me in the hospital, then once I was home with my son, called to see if it was okay for her and another co-worker to stop by to see us. Permission was granted. My only concern was the well-being of my newborn son; I wasn't thinking about makeup.

When they arrived, I opened the door, barefaced and all.

"Girl, what happened to your face? Do you need me to hurt your husband for you?" my other colleague said.

We all laughed before I explained the accident and why she never saw it before. I was slightly irritated; this was the attention I worked years to avoid.

"Oh, ok I just wanted to make sure you weren't in an abusive relationship where you need me to help you out," she continued. Eventually, the focus was taken off of me and placed on the baby, where I wanted it to be all along.

Once my maternity leave ended and I returned to work, a few other colleagues wove themselves into my life, making me feel vulnerable yet again; I decided to share my story with them. When I showed them my scar, their reactions were uneventful. They listened to my story, encouraged and accepted me. To this day, I can still hear one of them saying, "You're beautiful inside and out."

While my co-workers may not remember these events, I do and I'm thankful that each of them played a role in helping me to become more comfortable with sharing my story. Their assurance built my confidence a little more.

When we found out we were pregnant with our second son, I wondered if I was blessed with sons so I could help them not to be superficial when dealing with women and others in general. Surely, they would meet people with scars; internal and external. I wanted to send my sons in the world as kind and compassionate human beings, ensuring they'd never intentionally inflict the pain on others that some have imposed on me. I wanted my sons to be better, to do better, and to love better.

I know for sure my experiences had an impact on my husband. One evening, after we settled in for the day, he told me that he encountered a woman who had a facial disfiguration at his job. Unlike my scar, hers couldn't be concealed.

"It was obvious she was trying to hide the side of her face." He was silent for a moment before he began speaking again. "I did everything in my power not to stare at her scars. I made sure I looked directly into her eyes. I spoke to her like we were old friends and tried to make her feel as comfortable as I could."

He said the longer they talked, the less guarded the lady seemed. His approach worked, and the woman relaxed.

"Now imagine how she would've felt if you would've stared at her face instead of looking her in her eyes," I told him. "Imagine if you acted awkward and didn't carry on a conversation that made her feel like nothing was wrong with her. I can relate to her because although my scar is smaller and not deformed, I still know what it feels like."

My husband listened attentively, his eyes showing a deeper understanding of my world.

"It's such an uncomfortable feeling having people gawk at you, so on behalf of that woman I want to thank you for being gentle and understanding with her," I commended him with a smile and a hug.

"Thank you for preparing me to relate to her in a sensitive manner," he said. "I understand why you cling to your concealer. It's a source of comfort for you and I get that."

He hugged me tighter.

Cordially Invited

Exposing myself at work helped move me further along my path to healing. I had an idea that would take me out of my comfort zone, while holding onto a safety net in case I needed an escape. I decided to invite a few ladies to my home to fellowship as an olive branch to get closer to the women who normally reached out to me. The gathering was intimate; my intentions were purely to make connections that could blossom into friendships. I longed to build a girlfriend circle, and was open to the idea of releasing myself from being a "free agent" friend.

I invited 26 women to the gathering. These were women who I believed were God fearing, positive, uplifting, and compassionate about life and the lives of others. I could benefit from being surrounded by women who shared similar ideas and interests. While these women possessed their own forms of individuality, in some fashion, they could relate or simply understand some of the challenges each person may have experienced. Together, we could truly inspire each other.

As I wrote my guest list, I was in awe at the number of them who touched my life in some manner. They ranged from people I'd known growing up in South Carolina, to those I recently met. I was creating an environment of like-minded women under one roof for an evening of enjoyment.

To my surprise, 19 women accepted my invitation. There was no turning back. I planned the perfect gathering; unfortunately, the weather had plans of its own.

The day finally arrived, and I was a big ball of nerves. Once three guests cancelled because of the weather, I was convinced it wasn't going to happen. The other ladies would probably call and cancel, too. Thankfully, I was wrong. Despite the dreary weather, I welcomed 16 ladies into my home.

The first ladies arrived at 6:00 PM; the last three left around midnight. We had a wonderful time! It felt good to bring so many women together to mix and mingle and share, especially those who didn't already know each other. In addition to boosting my comfort and peace, I successfully connected other positive women to each other, who exchanged contact information and planned to connect again.

I admit, the enlightening part wasn't the event itself, but what happened during planning it. The number of ladies who exposed their anxiety and discomfort was astonishing. Some of them even expressed they needed this positive *girl*'s night, but were simultaneously afraid to extend themselves. Like me, they ordinarily stayed to themselves. A few even mentioned they weren't sure if they'd fit in. According to them, other women their age seemed to have it all together, and they were uncomfortable being around people who were more "put together" than themselves. I listened in amazement, relating to some of what they were saying. Their transparency spoke to how they must've thought of me, too. If they believed the only people I interacted with were well "put together", then I must have been the same in their eyes. Remember, many of these women were strangers to one another, so their assumptions were solely based on what they assumed my guest list looked like. It was eye-opening to see how their fears emulated much of my own.

I wasn't alone.

One conversation that night really blessed me.

"I truly see you as someone who could become a real friend," one of the ladies said to me.

I knew what she meant by a "real friend", so I wasn't the least bit offended. She and I conversed on many occasions, but we didn't hang out or share in depth conversations about our lives with each other.

"I agree," I said.

I smiled; hers faded.

"I feel like I'm keeping a secret from you," she continued. "I want to tell you about what I've been doing in my free time and my aspirations for my future."

I listened intently as she shared a portion of her world with me, but the entire time she spoke, I couldn't stop the word *secret* from blaring through my mind. She felt guilty about hiding a secret from me without knowing I was hiding one from her and the other ladies. No one in that room knew about my scars and how they controlled me. My guest from South Carolina was aware of my physical scar, but she hadn't seen me in over 20 years, and may not have remembered.

After we finished speaking, I thought about confessing my secret. I contemplated admitting my struggles and how I planned to overcome them to everyone. I could've informed them of the huge role they were currently playing in helping me to release my fears of allowing people to get too close to me.

I could have, but I didn't.

Remember, I was taking baby steps. Step one was opening my home and surrounding myself with women who I discovered were more like me than I thought. Step two, was unveiling myself at some point and allowing them to see me. All of me. I believed wholeheartedly these amazing women would fully support me; my circle of women who held power they had yet to know about.

Aside from writing and encouraging myself, I began sharing with people what I was going through to advance the healing process. After spending time mulling over how I would start, one day I just did it.

The first woman I confided in was a guest from girls' night.

"Hey, do you have a moment to chat in private?" I asked her.

"Sure, is everything ok?" she looked concerned.

I assured her everything was fine, and we found a quiet place to talk. "I have something extremely personal to tell you," I said, immediately ripping the Band-aid. She leaned in close to me, anticipating my next words.

I dumped my story on her, unable to control the tears that fell as I recounted my pain. Her reaction was filled with mixed emotions. She told me how special she felt that I shared my scars - which she never noticed. What surprised her was my emotional damage.

"I'm proud of you," she beamed. "I'm humbled that you would trust me with this."

My heart pounded through my chest. I was filled with fear, anxiety, nervousness, doubt, and embarrassment; everything Satan wants us to feel. But the more I opened up, calm and confidence came over me. I felt safe and vulnerable; just as God expects us to be. Regardless of how great I was beginning to feel, I was so excited that moment was over.

A few days later, I went for it again.

I was able to lay my scars out and be vulnerable with another attendee from the party. She and I had known each other for many years. As I built up the nerve to share my story, she incorrectly assumed I was suffering from an illness. I suppose it was the suspenseful way I approached her. But once I spilled my heart, she confirmed what my husband had told me for years.

You do know people can still see your scar even though you have on concealer, right?

"I have noticed it, but never knew exactly what it was and never asked," she confirmed.

"When do you think you noticed it?"

"When we met 16 years ago," she said. "We all have our scars, and if people can't accept you because of your scar then you don't need them in your life anyway."

Confiding in my new circle gave me even more courage to continue opening up to others. Everyone I spoke to was positive and encouraging.

The healing process had begun.

Fresh Outlook

Like most changes in life, I needed a system to balance the ups and downs I was experiencing. I craved motivation; it's important to know what works for you. I developed a system that helped me through it, taking steps which worked for me.

I love cake.

I love several kinds of cake actually, but Red Velvet holds a special place in my stomach. If you know anything about baking, then you know that one of the most important steps all bakers take is to sift the flour. The purpose of sifting is to remove lumps and make it easier to mix with the other ingredients. Well, just like with baking, I decided in order to truly celebrate myself, I must learn to SIFT. I needed to sift through life by changing my outlook on how I perceived myself. Once I caught that revelation, whenever I felt less than who I am or not good enough, I reminded myself to S.I.F.T.:

Stop, Internalizing, Foolish, Thoughts.

Negative thoughts are just that - foolish.

It shouldn't have mattered that in a room full of people, I was the only person with a burn mark. What mattered the most was that I was there. If someone didn't value who I am as a person or what I had to offer as an individual, friend, colleague, or fellow group member, then that was their issue not mine. I am who I am. It was time for me to S.I.F.T. through all those years of hurt. I needed to S.I.F.T. through my experiences and decipher what was true and relevant.

If I had known better, I would've put on my big girl undies and poked my chest out each time anyone attempted to make me feel inadequate or any time my brain told me something negative. That was nothing but the work of the devil. The thoughts I had caused me to lay low and isolate myself from people; I learned how to play it safe. But now, I refuse to feed into those ridiculous unfounded thoughts anymore. I will S.I.F.T. and change my life for the better. I will work to become the best version of myself.

We are what we believe. If you believe in yourself and the gifts God has blessed you with, and use them to empower others and yourself, then you are unstoppable. I am unstoppable. I must remember this and live in such a way which allows me to not only speak, but believe positive words.

I was dancing to a new tune. I love to dance, which was why it was so fitting that BOOGIE became my other acronym for life.

Be **O**pen! **O**thers **G**ive **I**nsight **E**very-day.

I became a magnet for others to confide in. Now, I wanted to reciprocate by disclosing my feelings with others, too.

People needed to know that behind my smile were deep wounds. I was a loner by choice; however, I could help others without pause. I just couldn't help myself. Very few people asked me how I was really doing. Truthfully, even if they asked, I would've lied and said fine, whether I was or not. My tune changed as I learned to B.O.O.G.I.E. my way through life.

God Speaks to Me

My writing mostly derives from personal experiences, but also comes through meditating and spending time with God. The decision to no longer hide behind my scar was not one I made hastily. There were many days I thought of turning back, thinking, "Maybe this isn't such a big deal. I just need to get over it."

When I dug deeper, I saw I was sweeping circumstances under the rug, which I have done too many years. And what has denial brought me? Unresolved issues which turn into insecurities and self-scrutiny. I am not seeking sympathy for allowing myself to endure so much hurt through the years without properly addressing it. It is my desire for people to understand the motivation behind my silence. In my mind, I couldn't fathom anyone wanting to hear about how an almost 50-year-old woman was imprisoned by trauma from childhood through now. But I realize and whole heartedly believe, there are others who are ready to free themselves, just like me.

Since I often serve as an uncertified counselor for many, why not cast my net wider to assist them? I truly have a level of gratitude for each lesson learned because I have found strength in each scar. It took reflecting on my life and the experiences that have molded me into the person I am today. I have also released skepticism, and the idea that my scars breed shortcomings.

Challenges aren't meant to be easy, so working on me will be a continuous labor of love in progress. If I am developing each day, my efforts will only get better. Closing open wounds left from the scars is a perfect beginning to healing. No more reminiscing on the days when I was hurt and alone. God chose me for every scar which has transformed me. I am choosing to turn on the power within and soar to new heights by no longer being a hostage to my scars.

We have all dealt with hurt. Whatever its form, the hurt caused anguish. I found that the key to dealing with trauma is acknowledgement and acceptance. Instead of focusing on feeling isolated because I am what appears to be different than others physically. Instead of intentionally separating myself from people because I'm scared of being hurt again, I accept myself for who I am – scars and all. My experiences that have left footprints in my life belong to me, by the hands of God. There is no time frame for dealing with war wounds. What matters is that we deal with and learn to embrace them at some point in our life. Self-pity is not a place to remain; it's not healthy or productive.

The healing process is like a puzzle; the pieces that come together are amazing. To put the puzzle together, you must go through the pain of reliving various events in your life...even the not so pleasant ones. I accomplished this through writing. It started by jotting my thoughts down in journals or random pieces of paper to release thoughts, feelings and ideas that I needed to get out of my head. Instead of saving my notebooks for no one else's eyes but mine, I penned this memoir, hoping to free myself from captivity.

Negative people in my life led me to believe I wasn't good enough, and foolishly I believed it. Unknowingly, I've been assembling my puzzle for many years; I'm so excited to see and live in the moment of the finished product. When assembling your puzzle, think about how certain events affected you. How did they make you feel? What should you have done differently to make this puzzle smoother? For me, discussing my scars would have helped me more. Not just talking about it, but clearly expressing my feelings. I guarantee there are so many who will be shocked to know I have been dealing with such heavy insecurities for so long.

Perfection

Several people I know - myself included, strive for perfection. I can't say I know many who want to be anything less than excellent. What I didn't understand in the past was how my goal of perfection wreaked havoc in my life. I couldn't see past my need to be great, to be amazing…perfect. Even seeing my admission in writing looks strange, because I never thought of myself as a perfectionist. But the more I've studied myself, it's become clear that I am one. Not only have I been a perfectionist, I expected everyone around me to be one as well.

"You have very high expectations and you're looking for everyone to be perfect," my husband declared one day. His assertion was a blow to my ego; I didn't see it coming.

Perfection: *the condition, state or quality of being free or as free as possible from all flaws or defects.*

Earlier in this book, I touched on how my scar had me physically hiding out of fear of not fitting in. I've also discussed how my internal scars caused me to build walls as a way of protecting myself from others – my way of avoiding relationships which had the potential of being imperfect. More than anything, I wanted to avoid unwanted drama.

Today, I can admit that maybe I do have a false notion of perfection. I have no qualms admitting that I am overly critical of

73

myself. Most people are their own worst critics, but I have the ability to take it to the extreme. The flip side to that is, I'm also the first person to acknowledge when I have failed or made a mistake. Taking ownership is something I pride myself on and a lesson I have tried my best to instill in my children. It was tough at times seeing that they were not quite getting it, but they are finally realizing that personal responsibility - though difficult, garners self-respect and earns the respect of others.

Now, let me be completely honest. Even though I was the first to admit that I was wrong or messed up, it still wasn't a pleasant thing for me to do. I'd get upset with myself and the *what if's* started flying.

What if I'd done things differently? What if I'd taken another route instead of the one I chose?

I shut down and blamed myself, trying to figure out what about me may have caused the situation to falter.

To my husband's point, as a result of my upbringing, I set unreasonably high expectations for myself and everyone around me. That would be my best educated guess, but honestly - I truly do not know where that pressure comes from. Most people are celebrated for giving, doing, and being their best, which is a great feeling. I know the joy that comes with being celebrated, as well as the disappointment of messing up. More than anything, I've always wanted to feel celebrated than disappointed whether it was at home, school, work, friendships, or relationships. For me, failing wasn't rewarding. Consequently, I realized that setting myself up to believe that people will meet my expectations, didn't feel gratifying either.

You know what else didn't feel good?

Putting so much pressure on myself.

I'm an over thinker, who's extremely hard on myself. I had to learn that even if I do everything right, sometimes things don't go the way I planned. Especially relationships. I can only control my part; what other people do is out of my control. There have been many times I made the decision not to allow people who don't have my best interest at heart to occupy space in my overcrowded mind.

I had several moments when I was going to quit writing this book, but I knew that was fear trying to get in my way. Fear told me to stop this project because I did not believe I was truly ready to put my business in the streets. I also pondered if this was the right time; we all know there's never a perfect time for anything. When I thought about the gathering I held at the beginning of 2020, I thought about the fact that I spent several years planning it in my head. A simple, intimate gathering took four years for me to pull together and work up the nerve to actually step out and do it. Most people throw weddings in less time than it took me to plan an evening at my house for a few ladies.

Bad experiences leave scars. Wounds are a part of living. I am excited that I have toned down my perfectionism to a point that not only do I accept my flaws, but also some of the flaws which exist in others – perfection is not required.

Lonesome Lioness – By Choice

I'm a Leo, but by now it should be clear that unlike some Leo's, I don't crave attention. In fact, I am just the opposite. It shouldn't come as a surprise to you that the following scenario blindsided me.

Obviously, I never saw myself as a model or as someone who could come close to strutting down the runway or gracing magazines. Other than my scar was the fact that I am 5'4 - well below average for a model. Nevertheless, I was surprised when I was stopped in the parking lot of a shopping center in Columbia, South Carolina, pre-concealer.

"Excuse me," said a young Caucasian man as he approached me.

"Yes?" I responded hurriedly.

"Have you ever thought about modeling?"

I smirked. "Me? No."

I wondered what kind of scam he was running, or if he was simply searching for short women with average features. He provided his information in the event I changed my mind, and we parted ways. Later that evening, I told my best friend, at the time, about my encounter. Her response cut me to the core.

"A model with a scar on her face? That would be the first."
Ouch.

I was too shocked to react and quickly changed the subject.

I never told her how insensitive and hurtful her remark was to me. I did, however, question myself, wondering if she was right. Was it impossible for me to be a model? Not only because of my height and weight but because of the scar on my face. I received my answer many years later.

My scar wouldn't prevent me from being a model, or at least coming close to being one because my employer selected me to grace the covers of pamphlets, posters, videos, and websites, on many different occasions.

With the help of my concealer, *I modeled with my scar!*

Heck, I could have also fulfilled my desires of being an actress or a television journalist - careers people told me were impossible to work in with my scar. Of course, those were negative seeds planted in my mind, but I believed it. I didn't see women on television with scars. And though at 5'4 and 135 pounds I'm not the ideal model size, I will hold on to the idea that I am good enough for any platform regardless of my scar.

While I have forgiven individuals in the scenarios I shared, I definitely have not forgotten the pain they caused. In most cases, I have not regained trust from the scars they left. I've concluded that for me, having friends wasn't all it was cracked up to be. Maybe I just never learned how to choose wisely. But I know I am not alone.

Several of you who are *"free agent"* friends like me. In fact, it was refreshing to hear some of my friends admit to not having a lot of friends by choice because of trust issues. I've lowered my guard through writing this book. I'm open to friendships. There are some amazing women who exist, and I look forward to getting to know them and others better. I'm becoming more diligent in creating my circle of trust.

My Puzzle Pieces

W hat makes up Denise?
Who is she in addition to what hurt her? How do her scars play in the landscape of her life?

Take my favorite color – yellow, for example. I love the boldness and the brightness of yellow. Did you know that colors can affect the way a person feels? When I think of yellow, I reflect on sunny days with the rays of sunlight beaming down, kissing my skin, creating happiness all around me. I think about birds singing, people laughing and participating in outdoor activities like walking, running, biking, swimming – you get the point. Yellow energizes me.

Usually.

It dawned on me that there are so many other ways in which yellow impacts negative vibes for me. Adverse feelings such as cautiousness and fear, can arise from my seeing it. Think about it: when you approach a traffic light that's on yellow, what is it telling you? Be cautious, slow down, and be on guard.

When entering a building and the floor is wet, what's normally put into place to alert visitors? A plastic yellow sign with a figure slipping and falling, warning visitors to be cautious because they may slip and fall, getting injured. This sign is bright enough to draw attention, and quickly warn of potential danger.

I never realized how my favorite color mirrored the dark points of my life at times. Is yellow still my favorite color, even after correlating it to my trauma? My answer is yes.

The beauty in this is that I have a choice.

I can choose to be on the side of yellow that is optimistic and positive, or I can be a pessimist, walking on eggshells in fear of past, present and future dangers. Remember, I am healing from anxiety. Therefore, I choose to renew myself and focus on loving me. Of course, this does not mean I will not take heed to any warnings or threats looming around. I will try my best not to waste time being self-destructive. I challenge myself and others to be proactive in choosing the path of positivity.

Not only is my favorite color yellow, but so is my favorite flower. I love sunflowers; I relate to them. If you Google most beautiful flowers, the sunflower does not appear, but it's beautiful in my eyes. This makes me think of the people who saw past my scars and encouraged me to be the beautiful person they'd seen me to be all along, and who I now see myself to be. Sunflowers have a unique look and stand out in any crowd. Their thick tall stems make them heavy, but also gives them strength. Sunflowers are symbols of love, devotion, and endurance. All the qualities I see in myself.

Many of us have a favorite color and maybe even a favorite flower, but I'm not sure how many have a favorite saying. For years, my personal email signature has read, ***Life is full of opportunities***. It's a reminder that not only is life full of opportunities, but what's most important is what we do with those opportunities presented to us. That's what really matters.

We can limit ourselves, or we can make the most of opportunities as I'm on the path to doing. I am so glad God granted me the chance to heal myself and others by sharing my story. We never know how something big or small can make a difference in someone's life. Take my email signature, for example. I don't consider it to be such a big deal, but people have paid attention to it, and some have even commented on it.

I love that I can help those who come to me in need. It's my love language, like the book by Gary Chapman. *The 5 Love*

Languages, The Secret to Love that Lasts. While the subtitle states the secret to love that lasts, I read this book with the purpose of applying it to myself and those I love, as well as people I interact with on a regular basis. I found the book to be beneficial in outlining the love languages of others and how they can be used in various relationships: romantic, friendships, work or casual. My takeaway from reading the book is that it's just as important to identify my love language as it is to recognize the language of others. Being able to understand what people need to feel loved, or if they need words of affirmation, quality time, receiving gifts, acts of service, or physical touch is paramount.

My love language is not words of affirmation. I had to learn to accept compliments. Neither is quality time - I'm okay with being by myself. In fact, when COVID 19 came upon us, I relished in the idea of not interacting with people outside of my immediate family daily. I consider myself to be an omnivert (both introverted and extroverted). I do love spending quality time with my family, but otherwise I'm alright being with me.

Next is physical touch.

Absolutely not.

Yes, we hug and show affection in our home, but physical touch still isn't my love language. Receiving gifts was not on my radar either. I love gifts, and it makes me feel special to know someone would take time to shop for me. But it doesn't motivate me.

Now the last love language - acts of service? Totally me! Serving is my love language. It is me all the way; hopefully you gleaned that between the pages of this book. I enjoy doing for others and giving of my time and energy for their sake. My calendar can be full and my body worn down, but I will find a way to carve out time, lend an ear and/or hand, run that errand, make that meal, or complete chores all to make others happy.

The next piece of my life puzzle is how I spend my spare time. When I am spending quality time with my family, one of the things we love to do is watch horror movies; my guilty pleasure. I'm not sure if it's the adrenaline rush gluing me to the screen or the buildup of suspense that takes me to another place mentally. Nonetheless, thrilling, gory films with high anticipation of what happens next captures our attention the most. I also am a fan of action, crime, and thrillers. There is one crime movie that never caught my attention or interest though. *Scarface.*

Having been called Scarface in a derogatory manner for years, the thought of viewing the film reminds me of the immature, unsympathetic kids and adults who found it appropriate to brand me with such a disgusting nickname. In fact, one of my sons innocently purchased a shirt bearing the Scarface symbol while I was in the process of writing this book. While I didn't overreact to him buying the shirt, I did ask a few questions about it.

"How was your trip to the mall?" I asked, casually.

"It was cool," he said as he strolled in the house with a few bags.

"Looks like you found a few items you liked. What did you buy?"

He reached in his bag and pulled out a white t-shirt. When he turned it around and showed me the front, my nerves twitched.

I calmly asked him, "What made you buy that shirt?"

"I like the way it looks," he responded nonchalantly.

"What do you like about it?"

"The colors."

The shirt had a portrait of Tony Montana - the film's protagonist, in front of a colorful background. Below the picture was the name which has always haunted me: SCARFACE.

"Have you ever seen that movie?" I nodded towards the title to avoid saying the name.

"No."

I decided not to share my disparaging thoughts about the shirt or the movie, which I'd never seen. Silence fell upon us; God intervened and gave me something positive and uplifting to focus on.

"This is for you," my son said pulling out another bag.

My heart melted.

"Oh, you thought about me while you were out shopping? How sweet!" I exclaimed.

Inside the bag was a rose gold necklace with a beautiful charm attached. In that moment, my love language switched to receiving gifts because his act of kindness really spoke to me. I pulled him in for a tight hug, silently vowing to myself to watch Scarface and get over it once and for all.

One rare day when I was alone, I picked up the remote, searched for the movie and watched it with an open mind and heart. I was hoping not to relate to this movie, but one scene spoke volumes to me. Al Pacino - as Tony Montana, was being interviewed by detectives.

"Where did you get that beauty scar?" the detective asked.

"When I was a kid," Tony responded.

His scar was on the left side of his face, same as mine.

Is that why people called me Scarface?

The movie was released in 1983, when I was 11 years old. As I continued watching, one line from one of the actors stood out to me.

"Every day above ground is a good day," he said.

That is a word! Not that I hadn't realized that before then, but I didn't expect to receive that message as I forced myself to watch the movie with the purpose of overcoming the negativity I associated with its name. That character's statement reminded me that I needed to be grateful that my situation wasn't worse.

Still Here

I've heard people advise that it's best to leave the past behind us and focus on the future.

I don't completely agree with that, because sometimes we need to revisit the past in order to remind ourselves how far we've come. Sometimes, we're resilient without knowing it.

Listen, I've been through a life-changing accident, years of negative remarks, an abundance of disappointments, and I'm still standing. None of it tore me down to the point of no repair. I am smiling and dancing for joy, reflecting about the life I have been able to maintain and live. I have waited patiently and looked forward for the day when I could allow myself to be at peace. That day has finally arrived! I am holding my head up high and ignoring anyone who ridicules me or utters anything other than inspiring words.

One morning, I woke up meditating on Jeremiah 29:11. *"For I know the thoughts that I think toward you, says the Lord, thoughts of peace and not of evil, to give you a future and a hope."*

God's words have helped me grow and trust in the signs He sends as a reminder that He's always there for me. He helps me S.I.F.T. through my thoughts. I must be obedient and keep God first in my mind, heart, and soul.

Today, I rejoice because I stand tall like a sunflower and look beyond the pain of my past. One of my favorite gospel songs is *Be Grateful*, by Walter Hawkins. The lyrics remind me that my situation could've been worse. I'm a private person by nature, but it's my pleasure to put everything in the spotlight if it means healing for me and for others.

August 2020, I celebrated my 48th birthday.

Normally, I go to work for my birthday and treat it as a regular day, but this time, I took the day off. Despite COVID 19, I wanted to relax, reflect, and rejoice about my journey. I woke up and walked to the bathroom, with a pep in my step. It could've been because I slept in, or maybe it was just knowing I was still here. I was alive, well and blessed to see another year of life. I thanked God for this day, as I do every day; I needed to listen to another beloved gospel song to celebrate - *Total Praise*, by Richard Smallwood.

After listening to the song and washing up, I stared at myself in the mirror. Tears rolled down my face as I thought about my writing journey thus far. I looked closer at myself and declared, "You did the right thing in choosing to heal. You did the right thing in packing the façade you have had for so many years. You did the right thing because after all, there is so much more to gain than to lose in freeing yourself from your scars."

Silence is golden, but in my case - silence was painful and desolate.

I am challenging myself and others to be better and get better each day. As mentioned, I am always busy caring, thinking about the wellbeing of others; now I need to begin doing the same for myself.

Once I finished cleaning myself up, I jumped right back in bed. I glanced at my phone, careful not to disturb the many messages clogging my screen. While receiving messages on my birthday is not rare, I never get to wake up to a string of unopened messages. I'm normally up early enough to retrieve them as they come in. This time, I chose not to immediately read them.

I placed the phone back on my nightstand, checked my emails and was greeted by an awesome quote: *Train your mind to see the good in everything. Positivity is a choice. The happiness of your life depends on the quality of your thoughts.*

How fitting to read this as I grew a year older on this day. I was on the right track, focusing on the positive things in life, understanding that some things were just meant to be.

This year's birthday showed me life is precious. Not only surviving during a pandemic, but a week before my birthday, one of my sorority sisters (my line sister) passed away. As if the sting of her death wasn't enough, her memorial service was held on my birthday. I loved the way my other line sisters and I came together to send her flowers and other items before her passing; some of us were able to visit with her as her health took a turn for the worse. Most of all, I loved how she enjoyed life to the fullest until her last breath.

When I finally left my home on my birthday, I continued reflecting upon my life and all the blessings that have come with it thus far. God truly listens and gives us the signs of confirmation right when we need them. As I drove around, I happened upon a funeral procession. How timely for God to see fit for me to live and share my story and that of others in order to help others. How perfect it is that I get another chance to live my life to the fullest by being myself, without hiding.

Equal Opportunist

It was never my intention to embark on this project alone. When I chose to share my story, I wanted to provide a platform for other women to share their narratives of emotional and physical scars. I am ecstatic that eight women have joined me on this journey of transparent healing. I understood many women I approached weren't quite ready to address their scars. I also realized that everyone's time for sharing will not be the same as mine or anyone else for that fact. With this in mind, I decided to allow anonymous submissions.

This platform isn't about knowing the identity of the person sharing their story, it's the experience they went through and their willingness to drop nuggets which may resonate with others. I connected with several women who believed in me, my project, and were ready to share their testimonies. It is my prayer that each author's passage will provide a clear statement that we all have scars and we all go through our own process of healing.

I needed to figure out the best way to solicit assistance from others. Initially, I only spoke with those I felt comfortable around - the people I introduced to my trauma. This approach generated a few responses from willing participants. While this was great, I still didn't have enough people to share their stories. So, I approached strangers who may be willing to join me. This seemed to work out great for the most part, but of course there's always one person who almost spoiled the movement. It was obvious that I'd struck a nerve when I contacted her, but the new me listened and moved on to the next. However, the incident was quite memorable.

Everything started off great with her. We exchanged emails and she provided her telephone number so we could discuss the project at length. When I got around to calling her, I was grateful for the long nap I'd taken earlier that day, because I needed all the clarity and energy I could get for the discussion that was about to take place. After exchanging greetings, she wasted no time getting straight to it.

"May I ask who sent you to ask for information about me?" she asked.

"No one sent me," I responded, flustered. "I'm calling to find out if you would like to be a part of my book project. As I shared earlier, I am working on a memoir. The book would predominantly be about the emotional and physical trauma I've suffered, which started when I was six months old and..."

"I don't mean to cut you off, but before we go any further, I need to let you know that I better not find out that anyone who I am not in good graces with sent you," she chastised me in a fearful, yet stern voice.

"I'm not aware of anyone we know in common," I stammered. "I'm simply trying to share my story and allow other women to participate in my journey. I'm sorry to hear that you are dealing with people who are hurting you or trying to harm you."

I stayed calm, attempting to let the woman know I wasn't a threat.

It was obvious she was not only dealing with the physical scars, but she definitely harbored plenty of emotional scars as well. I wanted to quickly terminate the call, but my compassion for hurting people extended her the time she needed to vent about the cycles of pain and distrust she experienced. An hour later, as I attempted to end the conversation, I began praying for her mental health and strength to move past her scars.

I eventually thanked her for her time.

"I will think about helping you with your book. I just need to know that you are not affiliated with anyone who is trying to harm me and my family. I will call you tomorrow once I have had more time to think about it and speak with my loved ones, is that ok?" she asked

"Sure," I answered, knowing I had no desire or intentions of speaking with her again. As painful as it was to hear her share what she had been going through, it was not the right energy for my project.

When we finally hung up, I immediately conveyed what happened to my husband with tears in my eyes. I felt attacked for being accused of contacting her for the purpose of doing nothing good or positive.

"Denise, you have to remember her story and experiences may not be as easy to discuss as you may think," my husband reminded me. "Based on what you've told me, she is clearly dealing with mental issues and needs someone to talk to. What are your thoughts from here?"

"I'm hoping she doesn't call me back," I chuckled. "If she does call though, I will thank her for her time and let her know it won't be in our best interest to work together."

"Good! I agree because you do not need or want any drama," he said.

That conversation was so harsh, it left me mentally drained. I could have easily gotten side tracked, but I didn't, thank God. I came across other women whom I had never met in person, that were excited to assist me with my project and eager to share their scars.

I continued on my mission, asking more and more women to participate. I went back to my associates and asked a few others. While some never responded, others responded with, "I'll get back to you," but never did. I kept reminding myself that everyone must open up in their own time.

"I'll consider it, but I don't think I've worked through my scars yet," replied a potential participant.

At least she was honest. I didn't pressure her, because I understood. She wasn't ready and it wasn't my place, plan, or purpose to push her to do something she was not ready to do.

"I thought about it, and now is just not the right time but hopefully one day I will," said another sister.

I thanked both women for recognizing the situations they needed to work through before they were ready to share their stories with others. Their hesitance was confirmation that what I'm doing is a big deal and necessary, because several women are still working through scars.

Weeks later during a conversation with someone else, I was reminded how uncomfortable it can be to have someone asking about your scars. I often believed that it was the lack of discussion causing me not to accept my scars. When I broached that point during a conversation, I was reminded that sometimes having conversations about scars can be a trigger for some people.

"Yes, I noticed there was something on your face Denise, but I just thought of it as a part of you and who you are," a friend of mine shared as we discussed my project. "I know someone who has dealt with and is still dealing with similar scarring and has always been offended when someone asks her about it, so that's why I never asked you about yours."

Her observation caused me to recall how I went through a phase of offense when people inquired about my scar. I remembered feeling uncomfortable, as if the focus was on my scar, not me and my many qualities that made me a great person.

After conversing with my friend, I went to a local department store and there was a potential participant for my book, walking by. It was a woman walking with two young ladies I assumed were her daughters. I wanted to approach them, but was afraid.

I watched her walk around, trying to avoid noticing the vitiligo around her eyes, near her nose and all over her hands. There were additional markings that showed through her sandals. I wanted to tell her about my book and ask if she would like to be a part of it. However, I could not shake the notion of feeling like a man who wants to approach a woman, but doesn't because she is with her girls. I felt like a coward. I almost added stalker to the list as well, because I found myself in the same aisles as her and the two young ladies as I contemplated saying something.

My previous conversation with the woman who accused me of working with others to conspire against her, deterred me. I thought about how embarrassing it would've been if this woman or those with her got defensive and went off on me in the store. I pushed that thought aside, along with all the other scenarios I could dream up. I stuck my chest out, held my head up high, and walked out of the store without saying a word to the woman. I believed that God had others waiting to share their stories and would work with me on my project.

And He did.

As promised, two days later in the midst of my prayers for strength and clarity, I found additional participants. It is amazing how many women are eager to share and help me as well as themselves. I love this opportunity to share such a positive movement with others.

Prayerfully, you will be blessed by their stories, too.

Submission 1 – Anonymous
"Broken Promises"

A *father is a girl's first love.*
A young lady should learn how to be treated by
observing how her father treats her and her mother.
This is what I heard growing up, but it's not my story.

I don't have a lot of childhood memories of my dad. He was in the military, and we moved around a lot. We even lived overseas for a while. Now there was a period when we didn't move for a while, and finally planted roots in a stable environment. The euphoria I felt was short-lived, though - Dad got orders to move to another state.

By this time, Mom was sick of moving.

"We'll stay here and see you on the weekends," she suggested to Dad.

Dad agreed to the arrangement and relocated, leaving Mom and me behind. He would drive back some weekends, while on others Mom and I visited him. The separation and bouncing back and forth eventually took a serious toll on their marriage.

When I was 10, my parents divorced.

I knew the divorce meant my dad and mom's relationship was over, but I didn't know it meant that my relationship with my dad would also come to an end. There were times I sat waiting for him to pick me up on his scheduled week. I'd wait for hours, only to be disappointed time after time.

"She's sitting here waiting on you," I'd hear Mom fuss on the phone.

He'd say something, then she'd hand the phone to me. I already knew what was coming, but I listened anyway.

"I planned on coming to get you, but your mom pissed me off, so I'm not," Dad would say.

I was numb.

I blamed Mom for pissing Dad off. She was the reason he didn't come - at least that's what I believed. Mom got tired of being the bad guy in the situation, so she did something she probably never planned to do. She showed me the divorce decree. The agreement stated my parents had joint custody of me. Dad was to pick me up every other weekend, and every other holiday.

...which didn't happen.

"Has he been doing anything it says in that document?" Mom asked.

I shook my head, even more disappointed than before.

By the time I turned 12, my life changed again. Dad remarried and had a ready-made family. His wife had three children, the youngest of whom was my age.

In the beginning, we all lived in the same city. I would see Dad every now and then, but not nearly as much as I liked. When I was 13, the distance between Dad and I grew, not just emotionally but physically as well. Especially as Dad was stationed overseas once again.

Before he left, he and his new wife showed up bright and early one morning. They were taking me to get my official passport.

"I'm going to send for you and you can come visit us sometimes."

I thought things were finally getting on the right track for Dad and me, but I was wrong. He lived overseas for two years; not once did he send for me.

Disappointed again.

Dad moved back to the U.S., but our relationship dissolved to nothing. How could we have one? He spent his time entertaining his new life and his new family. It was painfully obvious he didn't care about me. That was when I learned that putting trust in a man would always let you down.

Scarred.

My life went on without Dad. I graduated high school, then enrolled in college. College life was stressful enough; Dad and I only spoke once in a blue moon, which impacted me, hard. Dad didn't help with tuition or anything I needed for school, even though I reached out asking for help with purchasing my books.

"Things are tight right now," was the answer I received.

"I'm not sure why I even called you in the first place," I spat. "Don't worry, I'll be just fine."

I was disappointed again, feeling stupid for calling.

A year out of college, in the midst of planning a wedding, my fiancé and I decided to forgo the ceremony and marry at the justice of the peace. Forget the bells and whistles, I was ready to become his wife.

I believed I was truly in love, even though we were both young and were still experiencing life. In the beginning of our courtship, I shared with him that I didn't have a relationship with my father. I was shocked when he shared that he didn't have one with his father, either. We empathized with each other's paternal trauma. Even though we had that in common - and part of me really did love him, I couldn't ignore the gut feeling we wouldn't remain married.

We lasted for five years until I admitted I couldn't stay in the marriage any longer. We never had children, because I refused to bring a child into our unstable situation. He would get mad at me and move into another part of the house. Days would go by without my husband uttering a word to me. He treated me like I was invisible; it was pure torture.

The final straw for me was when my Grandfather passed away and the man I was married to wasn't there for me.

Disappointed by a man once again.

Why am I here with you when you're not there for me when I need you the most?

I pondered that question long and hard. There came a point when I had no choice but to answer my own question. I didn't have to be there. I didn't need him, when I could do for myself.

There I was again, experiencing disappointment at the hands of a male who should've loved and cared for me.

Scarred.

Today, I'm approaching my 19th year of being divorced. Throughout the years, I've dated a few times, but my scars prevented me from leaping into another serious relationship. I have given my all to my career, instead of entertaining relationships. Part of me wonders if I will ever find my true soulmate. And if I do, will I ever fully trust a man?

I want nothing more than to fall head over heels in love and trust the man I've chosen to spend my time and life with. But the thought of handing over my heart to a man again is scary for me. This is a sad predicament to be in, especially in my late forties. But deep down inside, I'm still that little girl standing at the screen door waiting on her dad.

Scarred.

Submission 2 - Santanya A. Mahoney
"Little Girl from Atlanta"

Antsy.
That's the one word left in me.
The one word I would use to describe my scar.

The vanilla colored nursery van transporting me to aftercare at a family member's house had no idea it was leaving me in the hands of my molester.

At the age of 46, I vividly remember the stench of him finishing on me, wiping me off, and instructing me to keep our secret. The secret was my scar; I assumed everyone could see it because I felt it...all over me.

As a child, I only felt comfortable in two places: my grandmother's room when she arrived home from a day of work at Woolworth (she was always happy to see me), and in my bedroom with my *Dream Barbie* House, flanked by my parents who loved and cared for me - but knew nothing about my secret scar.

In fifth grade, I confessed to my family that I had been molested. Their reaction made me want to vomit; I was told to get past it. In my mind, three seeds were planted that day: 1) Never have children you can't protect, 2) Open the door so wide, your children can talk to you about anything, and 3) Always be a safe space for kids.

Somewhere in my six-year-old mind, my scar led me to believe it was my job to protect my younger sister. I spent the last 40 years of my life believing I was her third parent. I don't blame my parents for my scar, but the trauma of Vietnam left my father too scarred to extend the best of himself to his girls. I respect how childhood experiences of varying degrees can impact our adult lives; mine impacted my parenting style to the extreme.

For years, I was obsessed with not having a child I could not protect. Eventually, I married a man who understood my passion for protecting children. I was fortunate to enlist my aunt to care for my daughter when I needed her to, before my baby could talk. Once she started speaking clearly, I immediately cultivated a communication style which allowed my daughter to freely and safely tell me anything she needed to express without being fearful. For example, when she broke things, did something she was not supposed to do, or just plain old confessed to a lie – we talked about it. Because I allowed her to be transparent, my daughter realized telling the truth was safe, and rarely felt it was necessary to keep secrets. Open communication with my daughter solidified my role as a strong mother, and helped heal my scar of molestation.

My daughter is the sun who ignited the healing of my scar; the rays of our relationship have drawn us closer over the years. As a child, there were very few places I felt welcomed, but as an adult, my husband and I have created a space where kids of all ages feel welcomed in our home. We are honored so many friends and family have allowed their children to visit us, kids have asked to move in with us, and parents have asked us to care for their babies if something happened to them. My husband's passion for obtaining every toy and electronic device he missed in childhood, along with my party planning spirit has made my home a safe and desired destination. To have children 10 months to 17 years feel at peace in my home…I know I am healed. With each passing day, my scar fades into obscurity, allowing transparent communication and love to burn brightly for me to bloom.

Submission 3 - Kimberly A. Walker
"Little Girl Lost"

I still remember the day my grandmother explained Jesus to me.

She taught me about Him in such a manner, I knew I had to have Him in my life. She told me Jesus was my friend, and He would protect me. What my grandmother didn't know, was that her six-year-old granddaughter had been enduring sexual abuse since the tender age of three and needed protection.

How do you ask your grandmother to protect you from one of her beloved sons? Was I a magnet attracting abusers to me?

The first time it happened claws at my memories like yesterday.

I was introduced to pedophilia when my babysitter forced me to search for candy she hid in her vagina. The memory tastes like puke in my brain; it's sickening to think of a three-year-old being told to put their mouth in such a place.

I couldn't erase what happened to me; I despised the touch of my violators, but learning to keep secrets safe early in life, I dealt with it. So on Sundays after church, my uncle embarked upon a five-year assault on my body in my Grandma's basement. I went along with it because if I didn't, he made my time there

97

very uncomfortable. I remember trying to stay up under my grandmother so my uncle wouldn't have an opportunity to get me alone.

Somehow, I still became his victim when my grandmother retired for afternoon naps.

Then there was Wally - the white man who molested me just shy of a year.

The crazy thing about Wally is that I would actually go to his workplace on my own, feeling obligated in a strange way. If I didn't show up, Wally would be upset with me. I couldn't handle him being disappointed.

By now, I had been molested by family, friends of family, and even a teenaged boy in the neighborhood. Being molested became a way of life for me. Not the life I dreamt of.

Why couldn't people just leave me alone? I felt like I had to allow them to touch me, to make them happy. My uncle ruined me with his manipulative ways; now I felt indebted to fulfill the perverted pleasures of anyone who put me in that position.

Eventually I spiraled out of control, abusing drugs and drinking heavily. Desperate to numb the pain so I wouldn't feel anything, the self-destructive cycle began in high school, lingering on into my adult years. I was a runaway crack addict, living on the streets of Cleveland, Ohio. My parents cared for my two daughters as I ricocheted between getting sober and relapsing. Even though I was tired of continually letting my family down, I couldn't stop.

Sadly, this cycle repeated for years. The monster I had become made me sick. I was damaging others as much as I harmed myself.

One day, I was ready to give up when suddenly, memories of my grandmother saying Jesus is my friend flooded my broken heart. I cried out, begging God to help me. I was exhausted, and hurting too bad to function. The world used me up. I'd been through and seen too much; it was time to call on my friend Jesus.

It was a sunny morning, and I walked to the corner of a street that never slept because of drug activity. There was something different about this day. Not a car or a person in sight. As I stood on the corner, I heard someone call my name, but didn't see anyone. The voice called "Kim," again – loud and clear. At that moment, I knew it was Jesus calling my name.

He was with me.

That was December 22, 2004. Since that day, God has done such a wonderful work in my life. I'm forever grateful to Him. Today I serve Him as an associate pastor of my church. I have a beautiful relationship with my daughters and son-in-law, and have been blessed with two amazing grandchildren. God gave me back everything and then some; I dedicate my life to Him.

I was once a little girl lost, but now I am found!

Submission 4 - Sharon J. Gathers
"Lupus Does Not Have Me"

I am Sharon J. Gathers, and I have Discoid Lupus, a chronic inflammatory autoimmune disease.

The immune system is designed to protect the body from infections. My immune system is compromised; it becomes hyperactive, and inappropriately attacks healthy connective tissue and internal organs in various parts of my body. Discoid Lupus also causes skin lesions all over my body when it flares up or when I come out of remission.

My journey with Discoid Lupus began over 33 years ago.

I was excited to be away at college, getting an education and meeting new people. College is scary; but what's even more frightening is being away from home, and your body goes haywire.

Imagine waking up one morning and finding what looks like mosquito bites all over your face and arms. Now imagine scratching uncontrollably, your skin hurting so much you don't want to touch it. It didn't take long for me to discover the marks on my skin were lesions. Once healed, the lesions left dark marks and blemishes in their wake. I was devastated; no one could convince me that I didn't look horrendous. I detested looking at myself. The marks made me hate going to class, but I had to go. Going anywhere else was totally out of the question.

I was in pain, depressed and filled with anxiety. Still, the diagnosis took over four months to detect.

I never felt so alone.

Emotionally, I was a total wreck. Vanity drove me insane; I was ashamed and embarrassed to be seen by anyone. Prior to this flare up, I don't ever remember being so self-conscious about my appearance. Often times during my pity parties, I gave myself pep talks in hopes that they would help me confront the outside world. Sometimes, the talks worked; more often than not, they failed.

As time wore on, I learned to apply make-up to help boost my confidence. A couple of times - with the use of a prescribed skin bleaching medication, I was able to rid myself of the blemishes altogether, but there was still the issue with my nose.

Prior to my diagnosis, I had a major flare up on my nose. Since the doctors weren't sure what they were dealing with at the time, the topical medication prescribed was basically trial and error. The medication caused the scab to separate and it affected the shape and skin texture of my nose, resulting in mass discolorations. For years, I fantasized about having plastic surgery.

Eventually, I answered my own questions during my pep talks without realizing it. Two questions stood out the most.

Will others be able to look past my appearance and notice the person I am inside?

I remember attending a party which I wasn't enthused about to begin with. At first, my marred appearance made me feel extremely out of place. As the night went on; however, I realized I was having a good time talking and laughing with people whom I just met. It was so refreshing. It dawned on me later how complete strangers were comfortable engaging in conversation with me. It was the first time I went out with my less than perfect face, and I had a wonderful time.

What a relief it was for people to look past my physical appearance! I felt empowered. There was no going back from then on.

Will I be judged for having a disease that I have no control over?

It took some time to get used to people gawking at me. It was annoying when strangers stared; I stayed in defensive mode because of it. I felt as if I had to verbally respond to non-compassionate people, but once I took time to assess their behavior as well as mine, I viewed the encounters differently. I saw that people don't know, what they don't know. From then on, I softened when it came to the curious looks.

Since then, I've relaxed and opened up more. I'm not exactly an open book, but I'm more approachable, especially when someone asks about my appearance. Believe it or not, I've learned to appreciate the questions. It's a win, win. Their curiosity gets satisfied, and I'm able to spread Lupus Awareness. My confidence has grown tremendously throughout my journey, and I have God to thank for that. Even though Lupus is a chronic disease and there is no cure yet, there is life beyond Lupus. God is always in control.

I Have Lupus, but Lupus Does NOT Have ME!

Submission 5 – Lodith M. Dean
"Embracing My Face"

I woke up to a day filled with sunshine and joy. My college classes were cancelled, so there was nothing on my agenda until Mom handed me a list of errands to run. I got up and dressed, excitedly preparing for the day ahead, unaware that my life was about to change forever.

As I dressed, I stopped to check myself in the mirror, paying careful attention to my face. I admired how beautiful my skin was. I thought it was pretty cool that while most young adults my age were dealing with acne and other skin problems, I couldn't even find a pimple. The irony of what I'd done by taking the time to look at myself didn't hit me until much later.

I left home to handle the errands, making a few stops along the way. My last stop was at a gas station to fill up my tank after a long day of driving. I refueled, and pulled out of the gas station as R&B singer Al B Sure, serenaded me with his smooth sound on the radio.

Suddenly, the music stopped.

"Ma'am, what's your name? Do you know what day it is? Who's the President of the United States?"

I was dazed and confused; the questions were fired at me, but I didn't know how to respond, or even who was asking.

How did I get here?

Excruciating pain surged through my chest, but what concerned me most was my face. Someone was wrapping me up like a mummy; why?

Where am I? Who are these people?

My eyes searched the room, until I spotted a familiar face. Daddy.

He was sitting in a chair beside the bed, worried. A few of my friends and family were also in my view, but I could only keep my left eye open for a moment before closing it again.

I tried my best not to panic. I probably would have...if I was able to move.

I left the house on Wednesday; I woke up in the hospital all bandaged up, on Saturday.

It took a minute for me to process what was happening, but it finally hit me: I was in the hospital, and there was something wrong with my face. I didn't care about the pain in my stomach, or my sore limbs or my closed right eye. All I wanted was to rip the bandages off and see my face.

After a few days, my family felt comfortable leaving my room for a little while.

I was finally alone.

I eased out of bed, body on fire. The staples in my stomach prevented me from standing upright, so I bent over and slowly made my way to the bathroom.

I found out earlier that I had surgery to repair liver lacerations. I understood everything doctors and nurses told me, but I was more concerned about my face. I was desperate to see what I looked like.

I reached the bathroom, which had the only mirror in the room.

As anxious as I was to see my face, I needed to prepare myself first; discovering what the bandages were hiding turned my insides. After a few minutes, I summoned the courage to look at my face, and almost fainted. My face – my unblemished pride, was scarred all the way into my scalp. My hair was shaved off to stitch my fractured skin; I endured a skin graft to create another eyelid because the original one was torn off in the accident.

Seeing my disfigurement was a tough pill to swallow, but I had to find the silver lining.

My life was changed forever but I was alive.

The accident didn't take me out. With that thought in mind, I prepared for what was to come. Was it easy? Of course not!

I used different products attempting to conceal my scars, but none of it made me feel like myself. I even wore my hair differently to help cover up my scarred forehead, but that got boring. There was a time I wouldn't wear my hair pulled back, but that changed too. I realized that although my face changed, I was still ME.

It didn't happen overnight, but I reached the conclusion that I am who I am, scars and all. I learned to accept my new face and I know that I am still as beautiful as the day of my car accident. I was still the young woman who took one last look at her beauty in the mirror. I was still her.

The change in my physical appearance also sparked an emotional change. My life would be different going forward but it wasn't all bad. I grew to love myself again. My scars didn't define me.

I learned to embrace the face!

Submission 6 – Makia Smith Thomas
"Owning My Scars"

I had a great start in life.
Wonderful parents, good health, great education, and an amazing social life. Everything seemed to go my way in my happy, safe, and relatively drama-free childhood.

Then…life happened.

The shift happened in my late teens.

Like most people, I struggled with wanting to be liked and accepted and slowly lost myself, trying to fit in.

I ended up in friendships and romantic relationships with toxic and dysfunctional people, completely obliterating my self-image. On the outside, all looked well – I attended one of the most prestigious colleges in the country and appeared to be thriving – but I started believing that I was unworthy of my blessings and slowly began engaging in habits that took me off my path.

Constant self-sabotage, destructive and irresponsible behavior, and shrinking to make other people feel comfortable became my norm. I constantly surrounded myself with people who didn't have my best interest at heart and made excuses for their behavior. I convinced myself that they didn't really mean the things

106

they said, or deserved a break because of their troubled youth. I genuinely believed I could change them, and it was my responsibility to support them in ways that no one else had. This mindset filled my life with constant drama and pain, leading to shame, fear, and settling for less than I wanted or deserved.

I became stagnant.

My detour to destruction wasn't the end of my story, though. Something amazing happened. My marriage fell apart, launching me on a deep and profound spiritual journey which changed my life forever.

Eventually, I started finding my way back to the old me. The REAL me.

This wasn't an easy path, but the reward has been so sweet. Through the years, I read tons of books, doing all the things I thought I was supposed to do to heal and think positive; but I remained stuck in shame. My previous decisions humiliated me, making it hard to move forward – especially because I had been given so many opportunities and so much support throughout my life.

For years, I focused on affirmations, setting intentions, burning sage, and meditating. I made significant progress, but I still wasn't where I wanted to be. After years of study, disappointments, highs, lows, pain, joy, tears, and laughter, I learned that the secret is in unraveling the lies I told myself, that most of us tell ourselves. Lies keep us stuck. Things like:

That was my fault and I deserve to suffer because I should have known better.

Good things like that never happen to me.

This is just the way it is…my life will never change.

The unfortunate part is, most of us don't realize that these subconscious thoughts are what really hold us back. However, doing the work to identify the core of your flawed thinking is an integral part of the healing process. The more I understood the concept that our thoughts create our life, I committed to eliminating thoughts and ideas that were no longer helpful for my spirit.

I no longer dwelled on what didn't work out, focusing on creating positive images in my mind based on what I wanted to happen instead. Keeping your thoughts focused on what you don't want, attracts more of exactly that - what you DON'T want.

I dug deep to alter my mindset, maintaining thoughts which made me feel loved, deserving, empowered and confident. I stopped judging myself for every misstep, and accepted that I was doing the best I could at that time based on the limitations I put upon myself. As Maya Angelou said, "When you know better, you do better."

Now I understand my power.

I am a child of God, worthy of all the amazing things life has to offer simply because I exist. There's no bad decision or misstep I can make that will make me any less deserving of this magic – it's my birthright as a human being.

The more I healed and grew, it became apparent that nothing I experienced was in vain. Now I use my scars to help other women grow. Had I not experienced the pain of toxic romantic relationships, toxic friendships, the death of my father, financial struggles, and divorce, I would not know just how magical I am. I have completely transformed my mindset, and teach other women how to do the same.

My late father used to say to me, "Remember who you are." I never understood the gravity of that statement until I started this journey. He is no longer here with me, but I know that he is watching over me with pride because I finally get it, and every day I choose to remember my power and magic.

Submission 7 - Stephanie
"Steppin' on Out Stephanie"

I was a pretty little light-skinned girl with long soft hair, who grew up on a wealthy tourist island in the low country off the shore of South Carolina. My privileged world was surrounded by beaches and pelicans; I was sheltered by my parents, who loved me more than life.

No one could have possibly known I was living a double life.

To outsiders, I was just pretty. Little boys stared at me during church services, shyly looking away with sly smiles when they were caught. They didn't mean anything by it. No one who admired my beauty did. But they didn't know I had a deep, dark, secret, that would soon expose itself for all the world to see.

At the age of five, my mother discovered a white spot on my foot. Upset and not knowing what to do about this spot on her baby's foot, she and my father shuttled me to various doctors seeking answers. Following a ton of visits, there was a doctor who was finally able to provide my parents with a diagnosis.

"It's nothing to worry about, it's probably vitiligo," the doctor reported nonchalantly. "It might make her turn ugly."

"Nothing to worry about and it might make her turn ugly?" Mom was offended.

"Yes - there's no cure for this skin disorder," the doctor stated matter-of-factly. "It won't hurt her, but it most likely will cause cosmetic disfigurement."

Vitiligo is a skin disorder in which the melanin in one's skin loses pigmentation, changing skin color in small or large patches. For some unknown reason, the body attacks its own pigment cells in a person's own body, dissolving skin pigment. Though I am the only person in my family who has this condition, vitiligo can be genetic. There are treatments that may improve the skin's appearance, but there is no known cure for vitiligo.

In elementary school, I wasn't self-conscious about the small patches that appeared on different parts of my body. I guess I was too young to know any difference between my skin and that of my classmates. At school, most of the kids just knew me as Stephanie - the quiet, smart girl; the teachers' kid. Stephanie with the white spots. Spots that everyone became accustomed to. It wasn't until I was a pre-teen that I really began to notice how different my skin was.

The white patches were more plentiful. There were white spots on my hands, feet, face…everywhere. What made matters worse was that the progression of these spots caused me to become even more of an introvert.

By the time I was a teenager, I began wearing make-up like my mother and big sister.

Thank God for make-up.

I was excited to camouflage the blemishes on my face. When my older cousin Alberta told my mom about Dermablend concealer foundation, I was able to bump covering up my imperfections up a notch. From high school into adulthood, I hid behind Dermablend. It was my mask. Behind this mask, I was a pretty girl again. However, I was still an introvert - shy, quiet, and nerdy.

One of my most special high school moments was going to senior prom.

I felt like Cinderella. I was escorted by a handsome, tall, skinny fellow whose personality was a lot like mine. When I walked into the building that evening, no one could believe it was me, Stephanie. I swapped my coke bottle eye glasses for contact lenses and wore a beautiful dress with heels.

Stephanie was steppin' on out!

Not long after that magical evening, things would never be the same for me.

My skin transitioned more. This painful process was emotionally and physically harrowing. Being brought up in the church, I didn't lose my faith; however, I often questioned God, asking Him, "Why me?"

I was angry at God for allowing me to have this skin disease. I felt as if I could not accept who God intended me to be.

It took years for me to totally come out of my shell. Once I lost all of the pigment in my skin, I stopped caring about the way my skin was transforming. I eventually reached a point of true acceptance of myself and started loving me.

My skin is now one color as I have lost all pigmentation.

I'm happier and more outgoing. I take an interest in learning new things while engaging in innovative ventures, as I am led spiritually. With God's help and the continued love and support of my family, I'm finally free from hiding behind make-up. I no longer want to conceal who I am. I am not perfect nor do I feel a need to be. I am a vessel with flaws, which represent the transformation into who I am today. So you see, I am still on the move. I continue boldly stepping out, and continue grooving through this wonderful life I've been blessed with. ...vitiligo and all.

Submission 8 - Shay
"Living in My Truth"

Growing up, I had a typical childhood. Both of my parents lived in the home with me and my siblings. Of course, things weren't perfect, but I had a home, family and friends and that was enough. But one day that all changed.

My parents separated, and I no longer had a home. My mom left my dad and we lived with my grandmother. I didn't understand why he wasn't around, or what happened to our family. I lost my sense of security and stability, and had no idea of the toll it would take on my life.

Nowhere felt like home.

Not my grandmother's house. Not my mother's house. My dad's house was no longer home. I was lost. I longed to have stability in my life. That's all I wanted. To have love, stability and security. But that want, that need for those things took me down a road I wasn't ready to travel. From rape, to teenage pregnancy and abuse, I'm fortunate to be able to share my story. I wanted so much for myself, but I went about it the wrong way.

I lost confidence in myself. I knew I was a good person, but my worth wasn't visible. I thought maybe this was what it's like to grow up. That I didn't deserve anything good to happen to me, because my world was filled with trauma.

I was 15 when I was raped.

Pregnant at 16.

Met my abuser at 17.

Life happened faster than I could process it. Before I knew it, I had multiple kids and an abusive partner. I honestly couldn't see myself surviving.

My biggest fear was losing my life to domestic violence. I kept telling myself I had to find a way out because if I didn't, I would die. Whether intentional or unintentional, death was where I was headed.

Eventually, a busted-up face gave me the strength to walk away.

It took complete hatred and fear that I was capable of physically harming someone to realize I needed to leave. I was getting closer and closer to death, whether it was mine or his. My kids needed me. My children feared for our safety and didn't want me out of their sight, because they thought I would be hurt or wouldn't come back at all.

I had no choice but to leave.

It was hard separating myself from that seven-year relationship, but I did it. In the beginning, it wasn't bad. This was supposed to be my family; my stability and security. I craved security so bad, I overlooked the red flags, ultimately loving him more than I loved myself without even realizing it. I didn't know what it meant to be in a relationship, and thought that because he wanted me around, he loved me. I had to come to terms that the relationship was toxic; the total opposite of what I wanted.

I had to let go and cut all ties. That was the only way I would be able to get peace.

Going through such a tumultuous experience taught me that peace is what I really crave. It's difficult at times, because I suffer from Post-traumatic Stress Disorder (PTSD) as a result of the abuse. Once I'm triggered, the nightmares, anxiety and depression come to convince me I have no control over my feelings and emotions. It took a lot to get to a place of peace, but I'm finally at a place where he doesn't bother me, even when he tries to. I've learned to block him and continue with our lives.

Since I've left, I have been in a much better place. Even my worst days are better than those I spent with him. I'm grateful every day for the strength to leave him.

I got everything back that he took from me, but so much better. House, car, job, life. I got my life back.

I became a self-published author of my first book, *Diary of a Broken Woman: Experience Pain Through Her Eyes*, which is a personal journal that I wrote throughout the course of that ill-fated relationship. My children learned how to be children, without fearing him coming around. Their peace made me work even harder because I needed them to be awesome. I vowed to give them everything that I craved. I vowed to make sure my daughters never fell for a man like their father, and that my boys would never become him.

I sleep peacefully at night, knowing that I am living up to those vows. It's still a process, but I take pride in my strength to live my truth and be able to tell my story.

Note to Readers

J eremiah 1:5
"Before I formed you in the womb, I knew you, and before you were born, I set you apart and appointed you a prophet to the nations."
I believe that joining me on this journey of embracing emotional and physical scars will be one of the best decisions most of you will ever make. I believe God intended for us to come together to realize how beautiful we are whether we're in or out of the storms that occur in our lives.

As I wrote this memoir, I thought about questions you may have as you're reading. I created this list that will hopefully clarify things in more detail.

Q: Are you seeking apologies from anyone who may have attributed to your emotional scars?

A: No, I am not seeking apologies from anyone. Though if anyone feels compelled to offer such, it will be accepted.

Q: Do you harbor any ill feelings towards those whose actions or words may have left scars?

A: No, I do not harbor any ill feelings. The memories have shaped me and made me stronger. Writing this memoir has helped me accept the fact that there are people who will judge me no matter the situation. If I did not have any physical scars, someone would probably find something else to use to criticize me. I learned this from one of my sons during a pep talk he had with me. I have also learned that it is none of my business what others say about me. I must know who I am and love myself, as well as my life to the fullest.

Q: Do you remember the people who aided in the emotional scars you have carried over the years?

A: I do remember who many of my "offenders" were. My guess is that not many of them recall their hurtful actions or words.

115

Often people who cause harm to others do not remember their actions. It is the people they hurt who are usually left to deal with the results. The power of maturity and forgiveness has allowed me not to hold grudges, but it doesn't erase memories.

Q: Why did it take you so long to get to the point of addressing your scars?

A: Even though I feel I am getting too old to carry this burden, I also thought I was not doing myself any justice by carrying these scars around. I felt that I needed to talk about them and wanted to get out of the "I must wear concealer" to "I will wear concealer if I want to" mindset.

Q: Has writing this memoir helped you?

A: Yes, I have transitioned through my writing. I love my God given scars and myself. This memoir has helped me to acknowledge that I have emotional scars and it has also helped me to accept my physical scars which was the first step to dealing with my emotional scars.

Q. How have you instilled confidence in your children?

A: My husband and I have sons who naturally seem to possess confidence about their abilities and themselves. It is an amazing blessing. Despite their innate ability to have confidence, we also maintained an open relationship with them. We ask questions about their feelings and their dealings with people in their lives. Additionally, we kept them involved in activities and in the community just as both of our parents did.

Q: What was the reaction from the people you know when you announced that you were writing a book?

A: Several people were surprised to learn about my scar, and others were surprised to learn that I decided to write about my scar and my feelings. Many said, "You didn't tell me you were writing a book." This project began as a private journey. I later decided I wanted to tell people about my scar and then realized that there was so much more than just saying I was involved in an accident when I was six months old. I took an opportunity to express myself and reach many at one time.

Q: What was the most interesting or thought-provoking question you have been asked once you revealed you were writing this book?

A: I was asked, how much money do I think I have spent in buying concealer to hide a scar that doesn't take away from who I am? I laughed at that question because I didn't have an answer. I wore concealer almost daily, but I did not apply a lot of it. One container usually lasted me for months.

Daily Pledge

I am claiming power over my emotional and physical scars. I will no longer conceal myself from the opportunities that await me. I will stop hiding and isolating myself due to my scars. I am beautiful, inside and out, despite what other people may think or even say about me. It is not my obligation to announce my scars publicly, but it is my responsibility to acknowledge my scars to myself. I love me and will continue to love the person God created me to be, for there is no one made to tackle the battles that belong to me. My scars are mine and my journey with them make me stronger. I fully accept who I am! I will not give up on living my best life and I refuse to give into my scars:

- I believe I am positive.
- I believe I am loved.
- I believe people enjoy being around me.
- I believe I am here for a greater purpose that I'm yet discovering.
- I believe I am special, with and without my scar(s) showing.

Go be great, ConcealHER No More – Embrace Experiences Not Scars!

Stay Connected with D'Author Nicole:

Website - www.DAuthorNicole.com

Facebook - D'Author Nicole

Instagram - D_AuthorNicole

Email – Dauthornicole@gmail.com